Kneelers

prayers from three nations

prayer handbook advent 2001-2002

Contributors
Fiona Bennett, John Slow, Noel Davies,
John Young, John Humphreys,
Meriel Chippindale

Editor
Norman Hart

An evolving prayer handbook

Once upon a time the London Missionary Society published a Congregational Prayer Fellowship Handbook to link its partner churches in prayerful support of the society's work (the 1972 edition was called The Congregational Prayer Fellowship Handbook in collaboration with the Presbyterian Church of England). When the London Missionary Society metamorphosed into the Council for World Mission there was a new understanding of mission. It was that 'Mission is one'. What were once called mission fields had become recognised as equal partners, there were no longer giving and receiving churches but mission in Africa, Asia, the Pacific and the Caribbean was on a par with mission in the UK. This had two consequences for the Prayer Handbook. One was that the content of the Prayer Handbook could no longer concentrate on 'foreign mission' and the other was that it was no longer appropriate for a Council for World Mission to produce a Prayer Handbook for what was primarily a United Kingdom readership. In 1984 the Prayer Handbook became a URC publication and its historic roots were recognised both by the inclusion of a representative of the European Region of CWM on the committee, and by the inclusion of personnel from European CWM partner churches as writers and editors. In 1991 the value of a collaborative approach was further underlined when each of the UK partner churches was invited to have its own representative on the production committee. This year the evolutionary process continues and it is highly appropriate that the present edition, which contains the work of writers from the three nations, has given birth to a Welsh language translation of the prayers to be published ecumenically.

Alan Paterson

Foreword

Writing prayers to be used by several thousand invisible (and mostly unknown) people is as difficult as preparing model sermons without knowing the congregations to whom they will be preached. The difference, I suppose, is that we do know the God to whom we are praying, even though very imperfectly, based on encounters with him which vary from writer to writer. In this year's Handbook we have tried to widen the area of these encounters by inviting writers from English, Welsh and Scottish churches to contribute, to reflect the concerns of the new national assemblies in Britain.

We asked for prayers for the three saints' days, and suggested that ideas of nationhood might colour the writers' meditation on the texts suggested by the Revised Common Lectionary. It proved an unfruitful idea, but some of the prayers are certainly coloured by the patch of land (and seashore) where the writers live and worship, the experiences of their neighbours and occasionally by their language. Though without an Irish church involvement in the preparation of the Handbook, we have also included special prayers for Ireland.

We have tried to offer prayers for public worship and private meditation, knowing that the book is used in a variety of ways. There is poetry here, expressing heightened emotion in the presence of God, but writers and committee have worked hard and humbly to try to make every contribution pray-able.

Your new editor has confined his contributions largely to describing the people in our local churches whom we can pray for alongside the prayer we shall be offering for the larger issues of our world in the year 2002, still hidden from us as we write. We have given more space to prayer 'intentions' for our fellow-Christians in the member churches of the Council for World Mission and those ventures which are particularly important to them at present. The order in which they appear follows very roughly the ecumenical prayer cycle of the World Council of Churches, though an exact match isn't possible.

The prayers themselves are this year printed on right-hand pages, for prominence, with supporting material on the left-hand pages.

The whole collection has the down-to-earth title of 'Kneelers', describing not only the support for prayer given by the padded floor-cushions on which many people pray but also the people doing the praying. You may point out that the church members who use this book don't often kneel, but most of us, in the words of the ancient carol 'Balulalow', bow 'the knees of our heart' when we turn to God. There is nothing to stop us using our other knees also, provided there is something to kneel on and we are confident we can get up again.

These prayers are offered to support the knees of your heart, in church or meeting and at home. Many of us lament that we find prayer difficult, but at its most passionate it is the believer's response to situations which seem not simply difficult but insoluble. Wearing another hat, I have before now been a member of a committee charged with intervening in just such a situation, where we discovered that we could do nothing but pray. And prayer works.

It has been pointed out to us that the prayers for the Sundays 'in ordinary time' towards the end of the year, where there are alternative sets of Old Testament readings in the Revised Common Lectionary, are based sometimes on one set, sometimes on the other and are therefore less helpful to churches following just one set. It was too late to change this year, but next year's prayer writers have agreed to follow one set of readings throughout the season.

Norman Hart

Say them again

The very best prayers from the Prayer Handbooks of 1986-95 have been selected by Graham Spicer and published as 'Say one again', available from the URC Bookshop at £5.95 (plus single copy post and packing £3.50). You don't have to leave the best of the past behind.

The prayer-writers in this issue are, from Scotland, Fiona Bennett and John Young, ministers in Wishaw and Greenock respectively; from England, Meriel Chippindale, minister in Sutton Coldfield, and John Slow, retired from fulltime ministry and in Wellingborough; and John Humphreys, Wales Moderator in the United Reformed Church, and Noel Davies, minister in the Union of Welsh Independents and a former General Secretary of CYTUN.

The kneelers illustrated (photographs by Katia Muscara) were designed by Naomi Hart to mark the 350th anniversary of Lion Walk URC, Colchester, and each was worked by a different member or friend of that church. They are used in the church's small chapel.

Seven days

Ideas for meditation and prayer on the seven days of Creation from Genesis 1 and 2, for use at any time of quiet

DAY ONE

Genesis 1:3   Then God said, Let there be light... and God separated the light from the darkness. He called the light Day and the darkness Night.
Vision, both physical and spiritual, is only possible when there is light. John's Gospel describes Jesus as the light which enlightens everyone in the world. He restored sight to blind people (Matthew 9:27, John 9:1) and criticised the lack of vision of the religious leaders (Matthew 23.24). In physical terms, the light of day is essential for all that grows in our world; for most creatures night is a time for rest and recovery. Yet many people work at night. Artificial day is created in parts of the earth turned away from the sun so that global business never rests, machinery continues to turn, people and information never stop travelling, the sick can be cared for, babies may be safely delivered, we can eat daily bread. A good night's rest is harder to come by.
We tinker with the clock in summertime, suggesting that we love light rather than darkness. We need both.

DAY TWO

Genesis 1:6   God separated the waters under the dome from the waters above the dome. He called the dome sky.
Sky is the air we breathe and also the air we easily pollute. The 'blood and fire and smoky mist' which blot out the sun in the last days (Joel 2, Acts 2) sound like our own sky when volcanoes explode, forest fires are burning and factory effluent is staining air, land and water. A hole has been ripped in the ozone layer which protects us from too much sun. We burn fossil fuels for energy and talk of reducing carbon emissions from our cars and our factory chimneys over 20, 30, 50 years. Yet air can turn the wind turbines to give us cleaner energy, if we choose.
The sky is also the fastest carrier of our communications, and we use it as parking space for a growing number of satellites, and highways for more and faster aircraft. Pioneer broadcaster Lord Reith saw the use of radio waves for nation to speak peace to nation. Jesus foresaw nation going to war against nation (Matthew 24:7). Our friendly sky is also filled with hostile messages and the weapons of global war.
We have come to depend on the crowded sky for our news, our national defences, our shuttle diplomacy, our entertainment, our holidays - as well as the breath of life. We did not create it; can we manage it?

DAY THREE

Genesis 1:9 God called the dry land earth, and the waters seas. And the earth brought forth plants yielding seeds, and trees bearing fruit.

This is the fertility that sustains our lives with today's food and tomorrow's crops. The earth cannot remain fertile where it is used but not nourished, where trees are massively felled and grasslands burnt. Fertile crescents have been turned to desert by neglect and bad management, but also by poor people's search for land on which to build, and fuel for their fires. Homes built and crops planted in our lifetime at the points where the land is divided from the water are under threat, or already swept away by flood. Jesus' picture of the man who does not base his life on God's wisdom (Matthew 7:24) was of a house built in a dry river-bed which is washed away in the next flood.

The Gospels are full of images of growth and dereliction. In Luke 13:6 Jesus likens us to fig trees whose soil needs to be well dug and fertilised if we are to be fruitful citizens. We are exercised by the need to feed the world's growing population; at odds over genetically modified crops; concerned about factory farming and single-crop cultures. The land is fragile.

DAY FOUR

Genesis 1:14 God made the two great lights, the greater to rule the day and the lesser the night; he also made the stars.

Sun, moon and stars are the regulators of our days and seasons, of our travelling, and even, some say, of our fortunes and our future.

Worshipping sun or moon, according to Deuteronomy - 'the second giving of the Law' - was punishable by death in ancient Israel (Deut 17:3): the creation must not be confused with the Creator. Malachi's 'sun of righteousness' (Malachi 4:2), though possibly echoing the winged sun-god of Egypt, has been seen by Christians as the rising Christ, our Sun King. We do not literally worship sun or moon in our enlightened age, but many are ready to believe that stars and planets predestine our daily lives.

The sun's influence may be growing, as millions in wealthier countries find the freedom to move to a warmer climate and take with them a more relaxed and maybe more self-indulgent lifestyle. We have discovered a mental health disorder brought on by too many days without sight of the sun. At the same time, those who have always lived in the sun find their crops more often scorched, their homes more often flooded from global warming and their dependence on the cool parts of the world still greater. The star which led the Magi to Bethlehem (Matthew 2:1-12) gave them no insight into Herod's world and his ruthless grasp on power. We still need reminding that these traffic signals of our world do not care for us and cannot rule us.

DAY FIVE

Genesis 1:20   God created every living creature with which the waters swarm, and every winged bird.

Those who are completely at home, as we are not, in water or in the air have their own Day. Fish provide major nourishment and an important livelihood in the Gospel stories. Jesus' first disciples were fishermen (Matthew 4:18) and even when they became 'fishers of people' never forgot their trade. John says that after Jesus' death they turned back to the Sea of Galilee for a night's fishing but caught nothing. Jesus, on the shore,
led them to a monster catch and then cooked fish for them (John 21). Fish is the protein in the feeding of the 4,000 (Matthew 15) and the 5,000 (Matthew 14). Fish remains the main protein in the diet of millions around the world, to the point where we have overfished the seas and made a scarcity of this most bountiful food.
Birds in the Gospels are the unvalued extras of a valued creation (Matthew 10:29) and the untoiling ornaments of nature (Matthew 6:26). Our world sometimes values them in the same way, for their beauty and their song, and sometimes shoots them for sport. Many of us count with concern their disappearance from our disappearing hedgerows.

DAY SIX

Genesis 1:25   God said, Let the earth bring forth living creatures, cattle and wild animals and everything that creeps upon the ground. Then God created humankind in his image, male and female.

People share the sixth Day with the beasts, giving a value to animals which we do not always respect. With no prompting from Scripture we have inserted ox and ass in the Bethlehem stable, but domestic animals in the Bible are not purely decorative, but the servants and helpers of humans. Balaam's ass is a pantomime animal, shying away from angels his master cannot see and finally opening its mouth to rebuke him (Numbers 22:30): 'Am I not still the donkey which you have ridden all your life? Have I ever taken such a liberty with you before?' Today we credit our dogs and horses with the same loyal and friendly instincts; and farmers who have watched their herds and flocks being burnt in the latest terrible epidemic of foot and mouth disease grieved at the destruction of treasured companions, not simply for their lost market value. Farming suicides have been an alarming loss to humanity as well as to our countryside.

A donkey carried Jesus into a palm-waving Jerusalem (Matthew 21) and became for us a symbol of the upside-down kingdom, the folly which subverted the wisdom of the wise. Our medical researchers face hostility and violence as they use animals to try to prevent human suffering. We have to ask how to understand the sixth day of creation.

DAY SEVEN

Genesis 2:2   And on the seventh day God rested.

On our seventh day (according to the airline timetables, on which Day 7 is Sunday and Day 1 Monday) we do not rest. We have handed over our day of rest, at the appeal of business and boredom, and are trying to live by bread alone rather than the words from God's mouth (Matthew 4:4). Jesus insisted that the sabbath was made for people (Mark 2:27); we have been persuaded to make it a working day, so that many have to earn their bread on the sabbath - and not by preaching. In his crowded ministry Jesus frequently sought solitary places (Matthew 14:13; 17:1; 24:3) for rest, thought and prayer. Often crowds discovered him, pleading for healing and for teaching, and he would not refuse them. Few of us are pursued by crowds - though maybe by work or worries - but many of us have lost the ability to rest, except fitfully on the evening commuter train or by the late night television. The church is proud to defend Sunday. Are we able to use our first day of the week as the Creator used the seventh?

*Pray with the **South Africa synod** of the United Congregational Church in Southern Africa (Africa pages in the CWM prayer leaflet)*

In Cape Town's Salt River, a working-class community that has suffered many of the abuses of modern society, the Salty Press is planning a new four-storey building and more openings for the town's jobless. It will offer fast printing and photocopying for passers-by, a full-scale printing press, a room for reflection and reading and a top-floor entertainment area. Already the expanding press, a Methodist venture which has had CWM funding, prints for a variety of churches and charities, including the HIV/AIDS Treatment Action Campaign.

Read Isaiah 2:1-5; Matthew 24:36-44

The readings for this week remind us of a vision for our world; a hope that God's Kingdom will reign on earth as it does in heaven.

Waiting is hard.
Believing in the vision,
where swords are turned into ploughshares,
is hard.

In an ambiguous world
        where one storm is calmed, just as another stirs
        where greed feels too powerful for love to conquer
        where old hurts run too deep for reconciliation
        where old dogs will not learn new tricks
        where scepticism is too pervasive,

we believe -
help our unbelief.

Lord of hope, we struggle to be your prophets.
Like them we fail to realise your vision;
forgive us for being too self-centred, too entrenched,
                too closed, too afraid,
                believing we can change nothing.

Waiting is hard and ambiguous.
Help us to accept that your kingdom may not fully emerge
tomorrow;
but nor should we forget about it until it feels more plausible or
seems more suitable to us.

Empower us, Spirit of life, against compromising
the truth, beauty and greatness of your kingdom.

Grant us the courage actively to wait in hope.

This kneeler, for deacons and those who do a similar job in looking after church buildings, shows a plumbline, a paintbrush and paintpot.

Pray for those who look after the business affairs and the fabric of the church. Business decisions may be easier or harder to make because the church is at the service of the Gospel, but they are unlikely to be exactly like those in the business world. Pray that they may know the prompting and the encouragement of the Spirit. Give thanks for those who use their everyday skills and strength to maintain a place for worship; pray especially for those whose task is made harder by poverty and vandalism.

*Pray with **Mozambique synod** in the United Congregational Church of Southern Africa (Africa pages of the CWM prayer leaflet).*

Though ravaged by fearsome floods in successive years, Mozambicans still find ways to celebrate life. The Christian Council of Mozambique promotes a dance group in Maputo which, three evenings a week and on Saturdays, teaches the country's song and dance traditions to young people trying to swim against the tide of alcohol, drugs and crime which surrounds them in the city.

Pharisees banked on holy ancestry,
What do we bank on?   Technology...   Wealth...

Status... Membership...

But the good King does not measure
by the Gold Standard.
His weights are justice, righteousness and peace.
How do we fare on his scales
as individuals, communities, nations?

Help us, good King,
to set your targets as our targets this Advent time:
to invest in and of ourselves,
to bank our hope in the good King's kingdom
        where old enmities are forgotten;
        where the mighty live peacefully with the weak;
        where the ruthless exploiters of the poor and needy
                are challenged;
        and where the vulnerable will be safe from danger.

*Pray with **Zimbabwe synod** of the United Congregational Church in Southern Africa and **Zimbabwe presbytery** of the United Presbyterian Church in Southern Africa (Africa pages in the CWM prayer leaflet).*

Churches throughout southern Africa are engaged in the struggle against HIV and AIDS. In Zimbabwe, with an infection rate of 28% of the population, people find it hard to admit that it is the underlying cause of so many deaths of people between 20 and 50. This makes Christian counselling more difficult, says Presbyterian Church of Wales missionary Janice Jones; and shortage of land for burials may soon force a cultural change as people have to consider cremation.

Read **James 5:7-10; Matthew 11:2-11**

The prophets waited for a long time for the new era to come.
Then with John the Baptist the old ended and the new was born.

In this waiting time, creating Spirit,
we give you thanks for the new life,
the new world which rose up
from the Seed which died.

We thank you for the hope of the Seed.
We take encouragement that over many years
the life of the Seed has spread,
wending its way across the earth;
flourishing where it finds welcomed space;
greening;
bringing new life wherever it finds root.

Help us to be good gardeners;
to recognise Christ's Seed wherever it grows;
to learn how best to care for the Seed;
to work hard with patience, endurance and faith
throughout the seasons;
to experience the pleasure, challenge and delight
of the gardener
as we nurture Christ's greening of the whole earth.

*Pray with the **South Africa presbytery** of the Uniting Presbyterian Church in Southern Africa (Africa pages in the CWM prayer leaflet)*

Charity Majiza, a teacher and then a theology student who was ordained in the Reformed Presbyterian Church of Southern Africa, became known early in her ministry for her work among South Africa's Tshivenda speakers. Made stateless by the racial politics of the 1980s, she served the Uniting Church in Australia before being recalled to her country to become general secretary of the South African Council of Churches. Today she heads the South African National Literacy Initiative of the country's Education Ministry, with five years in which to reduce the total of 3.5 million illiterate and innumerate people in rural and informal settlements.

A bodhran

Read Romans 1:1-7; Matthew 1:18-25

To be read in 2 groups of voices with pace and enthusiasm working up to a triumphant crescendo!
A tambourine or bodhran could keep the rhythm and a rehearsal may be useful.

(whisper)

pp	1	Good news! Good news!
	2	For you and for me
	1	Good news! Good news!
p	2	For towns and for nations
	1	Good news! Good news!
	2	God is on our side
mp	1	Good news! Good news!
(louder)	2	A Saviour is coming
	1	Good news! Good news!
	2	A child will be born
f		
	1	A royal child
	2	A wise and just leader
	1	No ordinary person
ff	2	No human power
	1	He is coming to save us
	2	From fear and death
	1	He is coming to lead us
	2	To joy and life

fff	1&2	Good news! Good news!
(loudest) SHOUT:		Look out, world!

Christmas has its own kneeler. The Lamb of God appears encircled by a wreath of holly on a background of three colours - gold for kingship, pale green for frankincense and reddish brown for myrrh, the gifts of the Magi.

O Father, you have declared your love to all people by the birth of the holy Child at Bethlehem: help us to welcome him with gladness and to make room for him in our common days, so that we may live at peace with one another and in goodwill with all your family, through the same Lord Jesus Christ.

Christmas Day

The excitement of Palm Sunday is due today with the arrival of the King!

Sound the trumpet! Strike the gong!
The waiting is over,
at last the day of hope has arrived!
God's salvation is revealed!
The Saviour has come!
He is a great being, greater than the angels;
Life is created and sustained through him.
He is light and life, the exact imprint of God's being.
The Son of God, the greatest
has come amongst us.
God's salvation is revealed!

(pause)

But where is the procession?
Where are the royal flags?
Where are the excited crowds?

There is   a stable
                a young mum and dad
                a baby.

Grant us, Saviour Christ, the vision this Christmas day,
to see and to celebrate
your astounding greatness and holy presence
in the midst of the ordinary and unlikely.
Grant us the vision this Christmas day.

'Muslims, Christians and Jews remember, and proudly affirm,
that they are followers of the one God,
children of Abraham, brothers and sisters...

Pax Christi

Amid the conflicts engulfing **Israel** and the **Palestinian** Territories, the United Reformed Church's Commitment for Life programme has a partner in the Palestinian Agricultural Relief Committee. It works under harsh climatic and political conditions in 239 villages to reclaim barren hillsides, to protect against confiscation; to involve women in establishing the security of the family food supply; to develop agricultural skills, and to create new products for new markets.

At a time of continuing crisis, pray with understanding
for the peoples of Israel and the Palestinian Territories
when violence and counter-violence drive them to despair,
filling minds and hearts with fear, mistrust and hatred.

For the fears of Israelis as the result of the Intifada
and a sense of national isolation.
For the fears of Palestinians in the face of
denials of human rights, border closures,
house demolitions, the uprooting of olive groves
and mounting hardships.

For the Palestinian Agricultural Relief Committee working in an emergency situation
to restore village wells as water supplies become critical,
to supply women with vegetable seeds, seedlings and poultry
so that they can feed their families,
and to market the season's olive oil at a reasonable price.

Pray not for Arab or Jew, or Palestinian or Israeli, but pray rather for ourselves
that we might not divide them in our prayers but keep them both together in our
hearts.

Read Isaiah 63:7-9; Matthew 2:13-23

We have arrived
at the other side of Christmas
and in your pantomime, God,
the scenery has changed.
We have come down to earth
with a jolt.

Joseph, Mary and Jesus,
safe for a while
in the shelter of a stable,
become homeless again,
refugees,
fearing for their lives,
seeking asylum in a foreign land,
pawns of political power.
They would be quite at home in our world.

How different from the Christmas story:
good news,
great joy,
glory,
peace.

But again we celebrate our faith:
the light shines in the darkness.
And the darkness has never put it out.

Move with us into the New Year
as we draw strength from
your faithful love
in a strange country.

'The (worldwide) Church's 420,000 foreign missionaries form a professional elite from the world's 145 heavily-Christian countries, charged with evangelising the world's four billion non-Christians in 105 non-Christian countries. But only 10 per cent of the total missionary force reaches these non-Christians; 90 per cent of missionaries go to heavily-Christian countries.' Less than one per cent of all thinking, discussion and action on evangelism concerns mission among the unevangelised.

Dr David Barrett of the Global Evangelisation Movement

*Pray with **Namibia synod** of the United Congregational Church in Southern Africa (Africa pages of the CWM prayer leaflet).*

Churches besides the Anglican Church in Namibia will be able to share in Christian teaching materials at various levels produced by two mission partners of the (Anglican) Church Mission Society who have just moved to Namibia after service in Russia.

Epiphany of the Lord

Read Ephesians 3:1-12; Matthew 2:1-12

What have we got in common with these wise men
(so-called)?
Who were they -
philosophers
politicians
astronomers
astrologers
scientists
magicians
kings?

Legend has given them names
and woven around them fanciful stories,
all part of the tradition we have been brought up on.

Perhaps what we share
is that we, like them,
are searching,
journeying into the unknown,
asking and living the questions,
touching the edge of mystery,
falling to our knees in wonder,
offering the varying gifts we have been given.

**God of epiphanies,
light up our pilgrim way
with moments of glory.**

The dove, the symbol of the baptism of the Spirit when Jesus came to John in the Jordan, is reflected in the water of baptism.

Pray for all those who bring their children for baptism in our churches, and for those who come asking for their own baptism. Ask God's wisdom for those who teach inquirers about Christian baptism, the Spirit of understanding for those who hear the teaching, and Jesus' steadfastness in the hearts of the congregation as they welcome the newcomers into the Church.

Read Isaiah 42:1-9; Matthew 3:13-17

Living Christ,
this was *your* decisive moment.
Rising from the river of baptism
you began to discover
what it meant
to be committed
to the way of the Servant.

In your moment
of seeing and hearing
the Spirit was preparing you for your mission:
you made the choice
and took the risk
of obedience
and the rippling reflection of a cross
rose from Jordan.

In your baptism
you set the pattern for us;
help us to know,
and discover,
what it means
to be committed
to the way of the servant.

May your Spirit
open our eyes
and ears
that we may become
partners in your mission;
and in obedience,
take up the cross and follow you.

Pray with **Botswana synod** *in the United Congregational Church in Southern Africa (Africa pages in the CWM prayer leaflet).*

Youth groups and youth choirs have flourished in Botswana's UCCSA churches in recent years and both are active in pastoral care in congregations, hospitals and the community. At the same time there has been a surge of young people offering themselves for the ordained ministry, who will soon outnumber senior ministers. HIV and AIDS, especially among young people, are a major threat to the nation's life and the synod has two fulltime officers mobilising the churches for education and caring. Several local churches run orphanages and most participate in home-care arrangements.

Read Isaiah 49:1-7; John 1:35-42

Living Christ,
this is our decisive moment,
when you invite us
to explore the mystery of who you are –
'Come and see'
        and
'Follow me'.

As we respond
and wrestle with your call,
our vocation,
we feel it as an extra weight
put upon our already overburdened shoulders,
so we are tempted
to ignore it,
or to run away from it.

Help us
to see what vocation really is:
the gradual unfolding,
like a flower,
of what you have called us to be
from before we were born,
from the foundation of the world.

God does not go back on his gifts or his call

*Pray with the Church of Christ in China's **Hong Kong Council** (East Asia pages in the CWM prayer leaflet).*

Changes in society and a downturn in the economy have brought hardship to many in Hong Kong. The Hong Kong Council of the Church of Christ in China is operating a short-term loan fund for jobless people and continues to maintain a family support service centre where pastors learn how to help the many who need family counselling.

Read Matthew 4:18-23

If only it was that simple, God,
to recognise the voice of Jesus,
clear
compelling
convincing,
enough to turn our lives in a new direction –
immediately!

If only it was that simple, God,
but those are rare moments:
most often
the voice of Jesus
slips into our consciousness
gradually
as we learn to recognise him
in the babble
and babel
of our everyday lives.

Draw us onwards
nudge us
encourage us
enable us
empower us
enthuse us.

Prompt us, disturbing God,
at the right moment,
to step into the unknown
sure of one thing only:
you will go with us.

Pray with the **Presbyterian Church in Taiwan** *(East Asia pages in the CWM prayer leaflet).*

Talking about a fair, run by the Kai-shuan Presbyterian church in Kaohsiung City, Taiwan, which had offered games, snacks, free medical screening and a flea market to the neighbourhood, group leader Chang Mei-yen commented, 'We must actively witness to these friends of the church, so they can see the glory of God in our actions and hear the difference between faith in Jesus and folk religion.'

Read Micah 6:1-8; Matthew 5:1-12

How wonderful it would be
if the world were upside down.
How wonderful it would be
if my thoughts were upside down.

Micah saw that an upside down world would be
a place of justice, a place of dignity and a place of the Spirit.
Matthew turned human thoughts upside down so that they would be
         full of celebration for the lives and hopes of others.

In the upside down world we would share and not grudgingly;
and our upside down thoughts would be generous and not suspicious.

**We confess to God that we are easily carried away by familiar and
powerful scriptures.**
         '. . . doing justice, loving kindness and walking humbly before God'
         'Blessed are . . .'
**We confess to you, God, that we say yes, our hearts sing yes, too easily.
We are moved simply by the beauty and hope of these words.
When our rejoicing is shallow, when we take refuge in guilt which helps
no-one, when we refuse your grace. Holy God, dare us to be your people.
Holy God, in Jesus you free us radically to turn towards the vision of
Micah and the celebration of Matthew. We thank you.**

*In silence bring, before God moments of holding back, from a person in
need of friendship, from a situation in need of a word of hope, from a
plea in need of justice.*

*In the silence home in on one of these for today. Offer this person;
these people, this place to God. Re-read the Micah or Matthew
passage.*
*Ask God to speak to your heart. How does God's loving-kindness,
grace and justice reach the
person or place in your prayer?
Talk it through with a friend.*

*Pray with the **Presbyterian Church in Korea** (East Asia pages in the CWM prayer leaflet).*

North Korea, from which most Christians fled to the South with the imposition of the Communist regime, has just two state-recognised churches and some 500 house churches. Following a visit to the North by its representative, the Presbyterian Church in Korea decided to give its own CWM self-support grant to the Church in North Korea. Initially the churches used the money for famine relief, but more recently the Korean Christian Federation in the North has used gifts from the South to build greenhouses and improve crop yields and food supplies.

Read Exodus 24:12 - 18; Matthew 17:1 - 9

Cloudy
mountains
are tricky and dangerous places.

And yet
cloudy mountains can be
places of glory, wonder, inspiration.
As Moses discovered, as Jesus' disciples slowly learned.

But
how do we tell
whether we are looking at
glorious presence or devouring fire?
After all, for Jesus, too, there was no easy glory:
glory meant a cross, devouring suffering, costly obedience.
But resurrection too: new dawn, new day, new beginning, future now.

NOW
gazing at
this mountain top
we see a glimpse
of what shall be, for me, for us, for all:
JESUS, 'for one half hour the way he always is',
Moses, law-giver, witness to Jesus' law of love,
Elijah, prophet, witness to Jesus, God's Word in human life.

For me,
for all nations,
here is good news - promising
transfiguration for persons, communities, nations:
their splendour and wealth brought to God's new world.

Drama lifts us out of the everyday to challenge and change our thinking and has its place in all worship. The masks of comedy and tragedy used in Greek drama remind us that drama in the life of the church can enrich fellowship and also communicate faith.

Pray that churches and worship leaders may recognise and use the effectiveness of drama in conveying the life of the invisible kingdom and awakening sleeping spirits. Pray for church members involved in acting and directing, whether within or outwith the church, that they may make a positive contribution to faith and truth.

Read Psalm 51; Matthew 6.16-21

Do you really know what's going on inside me, Lord?
It isn't as straightforward as you'd hope!
I can feel really bad about some of the things going on in my head and heart.
Other things, aren't so bad. Sometimes I quite surprise myself.
Some of the surprises are pleasing, some are not.
I guess you're pleased, Lord, sometimes, and often not.

I know Ash Wednesday is the day for repentance, getting ready for Lent.
The day of confession.
The day for such a mega-confession that there's nothing left to be salvaged.
It is me that's all wrong, and it's all of us that are all wrong!

Did Jesus make people feel bad for the sake of it? Was that his plan?
Religious professionals did enough of that.
Jesus challenged us to see ourselves and others differently, more lovingly
and less pedantically.
He wanted people on friendly terms with You and themselves.
He said to so many, 'so this is who you are, imagine who God can see you
becoming'.

This Ash Wednesday I'm not just going to make a list of what I,
my community and our world have got wrong.
This Ash Wednesday I'm going to think about just one or two situations in
my life, in our world that bother You.
I'm going to imagine how Jesus would talk to me about them,
how he would talk to us about them.
What parables or stories Jesus might tell to help us see things
from Your holy perspective.
It'll be uncomfortable. I'll have to be honest with him.
I know that there will be confession more profound
than any list I might come up with on my own.
And I know that he will help me move on.
Thanks be to God.

Pray with **Gereja Presbyterian Malaysia** *(East Asia pages in the CWM prayer leaflet).*

To prevent Christian students in Kuala Lumpur drifting from the faith and to share the gospel with non-Christian ones, the Revd Wong Fong Yang of Gereja Presbyterian Malaysia has started a new congregation in an area of the city close to the three main university colleges, which host over 80,000 students.

Lent 1

Read Genesis 2:15-17, 3:1-7; Matthew 4:1-11

Voice 1
Not Eden again, Lord!
I'm tired of its dubious tale about human beginnings,
gullible Adam giving way to the serpent's taunts.
Surely now we know better!
15 billion years of cosmic history put us in our place:
we are just one small episode in the story of being,
a story with a beginning and end we cannot yet imagine:
from big bang to big crunch? Lord, do you know the ending?

Voice 2
Listen, my child, Adam is not some primeval first man.
Adam is everyone, Eve is everyone;
the generations of humanity.
Adam is you, Eve is you,
struggling against evil, grasping for good,
always the promise of what is posslble,
always the fear of failure to be what we could become.

Voice 1
So, into our story Jesus came,
sharing our beginnings and endings,
knowing the temptations of desert places,
struggling against evil, grasping for good,
the final promise of what is possible - now and in the end.

**Lord, in our wilderness struggles today teach us:
that there are no quick fixes to turn the stones of
economic injustice into bread for all; that shaping
a more just future means becoming co-workers with
you, taking risks for a better world; that the destiny
of nations lies not in power or coercion but in humble
homage to you, the Lord of all. In Adam ALL died,
but in Christ ALL shall be made alive.**

Pray with **the Presbyterian Church in Singapore** *(East Asia pages of the CWM prayer leaflet).*

以爱联系
用心服事

Reduced in English to 'united in love and service', this Mandarin Chinese expression contains four characters meaning 'using love to build relationships' and four meaning 'diligent in service'. It has been chosen as the Presbyterian Church in Singapore's theme for the next three to five years.

Read **Genesis 12:I-4a; John 3:1-17**

Abram faithfully leaves his home.
 This has long been a story of faithful trust in God.
  He becomes Abraham, the father of many,
    sometimes warring, nations -
     Jewish, Muslim and Christian.
       Was that your intention, Holy God?

        Nicodemus talks with Jesus on being born again.
         Only being born of the Spirit counts.
           Yet not all 'spirit' is the Spirit, there's
             religious beauty and bigotry.
               Is it the throw of a dice?

              Abram set off, that's the point.
             Nicodemus begins to explore.
        It's the questing. It's the openness to tomorrow.
      It's the knowing that the Creator alone can create.

There is no arrival that we can judge complete.
   There is no thought that we can call whole.
      There is no moment from which holiness cannot flow.
         Life is not stagnant. God calls us to tomorrow.

**Holy God, we want to know and to be in charge. We want to
know that you know and that all will be well. And we'd like it
well in the way we'd like.**

**Grant us the wisdom to see our todays as instruments for
creating your tomorrows;**
and that the tomorrows we create are but stepping stones.
**Keep us journeying in life with a sense of expectation. May the
journeys, which are life, never be marred by our thinking we've
arrived. And may the arrivals always begin tomorrow's journey.**

Remember in your prayers those who serve the church in administration, in central offices, district and synod offices. Give thanks for faithful service and dedicated competence, much of it spanning many years. Ask that those whose service is sacrificial may find delight in giving it. Remember the national and ecumenical responsibilities of the leaders of churches, and the pastoral responsibility for ministers and congregations carried by the leaders of presbyteries and synods; that they may find God's yoke easy, and his burden light.

Dydd Gŵyl Dewi*

St David's Day

Read Isaiah 61:1-3; Hebrews 11:32-12:2; Matthew 5:13-16

Lord, we're never too sure about saints:
they seem so distant, so far away, so other-wordly.
How can Dewi speak to us today after fifteen centuries?

Even so, today we celebrate Dewi: monk, ascetic,
evangelist; building community, offering hospitality,
shaping culture: icon of what we could be.

In Wales, in the community of nations, we confess our
failure to learn from Dewi lessons for today's world - torn,
inhospitable, fragmented.
Lord, may your forgiveness make us whole again.

May the Spirit which anointed Dewi anoint us and send us
out like him:

> to announce good news
> to bind the broken-hearted
> to proclaim liberty to captives
> to announce your favour and vengeance

so that in Wales, in the community of nations,
your reign may flourish.

Lord, awaken the depths of our being to the presence and
power of Dewi and all the saints;
enfold us within the communion of saints,
surprise us with their vision of heaven.
Surrounded by such a cloud of witnesses:
let us look again towards Jesus, pioneer and perfecter of
faith - for them, for us, for all.
Let us be salt to restore joy of gladness instead of tears;
let us be light to bring hope, splendour for heavy hearts.
Like Dewi.

*St David's Day (Dewi=David)

Fellowship circles, often by age-groups - mothers and toddlers, men's groups, older women of a church 'generation' - are a help in building friendship within the congregation and sometimes a point of entry for newcomers. The hands of fellowship are linked around a cup of tea.

Pray for those who find the fellowship of the church most deeply in a circle of likeminded friends. Pray that they may be outward-looking for others who might welcome such a warm circle, and eager for the life and witness of the whole church. Regular house-groups, especially for fixed periods such as Lent, can be as supportive for many people as the whole church at worship and are a place for Christian education. Some churches run regular walking-parties for those who can walk and talk at the same time. Remember them all.

*Pray with the **Congregational Federation** in Britain (Europe pages in the CWM prayer leaflet).*

Congregational churches with a fresh approach to worship and outreach were encountered by Congregational Union of New Zealand general secretary Bob Franklyn when he visited Britain recently. In Hope, he found a church which formerly he had seen in decline set out cafe-style to give an informal feel to worship for the 60 adults and 40 children he met. In Taunton the Congregational Federation runs a cyber-cafe where young people browse the internet and have soft drinks - a friendly alternative to the week-end pub scene.

Read John 4:5-42

'Got any change pal?'
drifts from the shadow
into my face,
materialising
with hand outstretched,
desperate for a drink
to dowse the fire within.

'Change? That'll be right,
here's five pound, pal!'
my feet reply,
as shimmying past
(my conscience on the move)
I leave him high and dry
to nurse his need again

What change is possible
for me, for him? None till
both of us know we
are thirsty. John shows
the common cause for one
to minister to the other
desperate for a drink.

Then change is possible
for you, for me, and all
who come to the well
desperate for a drink of
life-giving water; for
we're not left high and dry
nursing our need of God.

God, together we come to the open well of your providing.
Meet our thirst with your refreshing, life-giving water.

Pray with the **Reformed Churches in the Netherlands** *(Europe pages of the CWM prayer leaflet).*

The congregations of the Reformed Church in the Netherlands are seeking to offer the Christian gospel to the many people 'shopping in the religious supermarket of Dutch society'. As political parties draw up their policies for the general election in 2002, the Council of Churches in the Netherlands has written to the main parties asking them to address issues such as social services for asylum-seekers, homelessness, ecology and the debt burden of the world's poorest countries, saying that 'unfettered self-enrichment' is undermining Netherlands society.

Read **John 9:1-41**

April nights on Iona
you can raise your face
to the clear night sky and watch
heaven leaking light
from a thousand sources
since the pulse of creation.

Surely Colum Cille's men
disciplined in prayer,
poetry, psalms and island life,
caught themselves turning
towards transcendent light,
drawn to the wonder beyond?

Keen wind, the machair beneath
brings each down to earth,
close to the immanent light
given to the seekers
who admit the darkness
which clouds all their judgement.

Far beyond, and deep within,
boundaries blur when
faced with the genetic light
which casts no shadows
of pride and tradition,
but pierces with truth and love.

Living light, dare I ask you to live within me?

Colum Cille = St Columba
machair = low-lying fertile grazing land close to a beach

A prayer for Ireland:

- land of saints and scholars

We give thanks for all who have found faith and witnessed to your love, Lord, through the life of the church in Ireland. We praise you for their readiness to reach out beyond its shores to take the gospel throughout the world.

- land of division

We pray for the people of Ireland who, over many centuries, have suffered through religious and political divisions. We cannot tell the whole story, or its cost in compromised witness in faith and loss of integrity in civic life. We seek only to learn form the story and to find a greater readiness to trust you and one another.

- land of violence and fear

We pray for all those who have been the victims of divisions which have led to violence and fear. We cry out for those who in their pain cannot forget and those who in their bitterness will not forgive.

- land of hope

We give thanks for all the glimmers of hope within divided religious communities as they find healing, and divided political communities as they find new energy to work for peace. Holy Spirit, continue to move in Ireland to bring a lasting peace that leads to fullness of life for all.

Bill Mahood

Read **John 11:1-45**

Lord, what were you thinking
when the rickle of bones called Lazarus
stumbled out to the light of day
bemused, half blinded by the glare?
> Were you trying to make amends
> for neglecting your friend four days ago?
> Shouldn't you have helped him long
> before he succumbed to his illness?
>> Was it tears of regret or grief you shed
>> as you wept openly in front of them all ?
>> Couldn't you be strong enough
>> to resist joining the wailing crowd?

Lord what were you thinking of?

I wear my unbelief like a talisman
against miracle stories which offend
my twenty-first century senses, and
try to awaken my awe and wonder.
> Yet Mary and Martha trouble me
> with their unqualified faith in Jesus.
> They knew, they knew what was possible
> for their brother, and spoke on his behalf.
>> Would I too not speak to Jesus for my
>> brother, my sister, more dead than alive?
>> Would I too not call on the friendship of Jesus
>> to raise them from death to fullness of life?

Would I not act for them when they cannot act?

Compassionate Jesus, act for us too,
for numbed by the death of what we hold dear,
wrapped close in the shrouds of pride and tradition,
we wait for your words, *'Come out and live'.*

Pray with the **United Reformed Church** *in Britain (Europe pages of the CWM prayer leaflet).*

The United Reformed Church's deputy general secretary, John Waller, has challenged synods and congregations to use resources available for the mission of the church (ministry, buildings, money) in new and creative ways. He points out that each URC minister serves fewer members than ever before, a fact disguised by the need for ministers to care for multiple congregations (and church buildings).

Palm Sunday and Passion Sunday

Read Matthew 21:1-11

Twenty centuries past, what city has not heard of your coming ?
From Bejing to Berlin, from Jerusalem to Johannesburg, from New York to New Delhi
surely the word has spread that you've come in peace, not violence
to enrich, renew, transform our lives, and bring us to shalom?

Blessed is he who comes in the name of the Lord. Hosanna in the highest.

Twenty centuries past, what city has not heard of your church?
From Catholic, Orthodox, or Reformed, Anglican, Evangelical, or Pentecostal
surely the message of acceptance, healing, confidence
in your royal advent, has been passed on through faithful living?

Blessed is he who comes in the name of the Lord. Hosanna in the highest.

Twenty centuries past, what city has not rejected you?
From penthouse to tenement, from factory to leisure centre, from theme park to concert hall,
surely the news is that this life is for taking, not giving
and what stands in the way of this lifestyle must now be removed?

Blessed is he who comes in the name of the Lord. Hosanna in the highest?

Twenty centuries past, what city does Christ seek to enter?
From leafy suburb to shanty town, from housing estate to west end flat, from salon to slum,
surely the sign of the church free from pride, united in deed,
must be the welcome Christ longs for as he enters your city?

Blessed is he who comes in the name of the Lord

Pray for local ecumenical partnerships and churches sharing buildings, trying to understand both the strains and the joys such partnerships bring to leaders and congregations. Pray that they will be kind to one another, learning from one other and accepting one another, even as God in Christ accepts them all. Ask that the whole Church may learn the lessons they have to teach us.

*Pray for the staff of the **Council for World Mission**, who service its programmes, its funding and its decision-making. CWM is a community of 31 mainline Protestant churches worldwide committed to sharing their resources of money, people, skills and insights globally to carry out God's mission locally.*

Read **John 12:1-11**

Servant God, I come to you this Holy Week
     needing to know more about
     what being a servant is like;
     place me in your company, so
     that I may learn from you the joy,
     and pain, of following your way.

Servant God, I come to you reluctantly,
     seeing the celebration,
     and joining half-heartedly, for
     there's a time and place for joy,
     and partying on the way to
     your cross can hardly be condoned.

Servant God, I come to you confusedly,
     watching you openly approve
     of the terrible waste of money
     involved in accepting her
     prodigal act of homage;
     for Judas, though a thief, was right.

Servant God, I come to you unwillingly
     for my ideal of serving you
     is not your idea of service,
     and the company you keep
     offends my sense of holiness
     and I do not understand you.

Servant God, I come to you this Holy Week
     needing to know more about
     what being a servant is like;
     take me into your company
     and teach me what I need to know
     in the imperative of love.

The Church is called to be a community which speaks to the world in God's name and speaks to God from the middle of the world's darkness and fustration. The prayer with beautiful buildings and lovely music must be a prayer which also speaks from the places where men and women work, or lack work, and are sad and hungry, suffer and die. To be near the love of God is to be near, as Jesus showed, to the darkness of the world. That is the 'place of prayer'.

Michael Ramsey

Pray for the fellowship of your church, that it may be open and loving, a fellowship which heals and gives strength to its members. Thank God that his Son comes to us in food and drink and that all who listen and lack are invited to his table, a place of sharing and not of worldly privilege.

Read John 12:20-36

'Unless a grain of wheat falls into the earth and dies,
it remains just a single grain;
but if it dies it hears much fruit.'

These powerfully awesome words weave through the events of Holy Week. They reach a climax in the crucifixion. Jesus dies in order that life may be celebrated. His compassion for the many folk with whom he spoke and to whom he listened propels him towards Calvary. His love for those who were marginalised by the religiously respectable within his own tradition undermined order and security, as well as the standing and power of which they were very defensive. This verse is about life, not death. Life in all its fullness is the passion of Jesus. He could not refuse to know, love, touch and respect people who were powerless and whose spirit was being choked by religious dogmatism and fear. The dying leads to a flourishing. The person and ministry of Jesus could not be held in check by death. His death is the extent of his passion for people; the proof of that passion lies in the miracle of resurrection.

Holy God, help me to recognise those things to which I must die,
the mere routine of church life,
the prejudice that lies unspoken and yet shouting within me,
the carelessness with which I read your Word in the scriptures,
the habits which crowd out spontaneity,
the fear of listening too deeply to my neighbour.

Holy God, you created life, you created me for life.
You offer life to be lived with celebration,
with joy and with love
for the sharing of your kingdom
for the speaking of your justice
and in gratitude for your grace.

Help me to live for, with and in you
freely, willingly and delightedly
reaching for the passion of Jesus.

Pray for the central assemblies of your church, that representatives will be thoughtfully chosen and make their decisions prayerfully and relying on the Holy Spirit. Ask for confidence and humility for those who chair the proceedings, who sometimes have to resolve unexpected conflicts and whose physical strength and pastoral concern are constantly called upon. Pray for harmony and unity of purpose among the assembly officers and committees.

Read **John 13:21-32**

'One of you will betray me'

me?

us?

how?

it's inevitable

and still Jesus offers bread and wine.

Judas was so committed,
he knew how he wanted Jesus to act;

Jesus knew well how
Judas was trapped by his own agenda;

Judas rushed to fix events which
were out of his control.

Jesus loved Judas

Holy Jesus, forgive me for not listening to you,
for not trusting your gracious path of love,
for trying to force you into my way
of seeing things, of being.
Gracious Jesus, let me receive more than bread and wine;
let me feel, deep within, your generous and patient gift of body
and blood.
Powerful Jesus, transform the way I receive.
Transform the ways I share your love within your world.

Pray for those who share in the pastoral care of your congregation and your neighbourhood. Pray especially for your minister and those who lead you in worship. Leaders can experience times of loneliness and dryness of imagination - pray that they will remember to call on the fullness God can give them. Pray for church elders, often doing full and demanding day jobs, that their eldership may not become a burden, and that others will minister to them.

Jesus washes his disciples' feet. Through this ordinary action he spoke volumes about the way God is with his creation: caring, loving and offering renewal and refreshment. Jesus serves. In this simple act we glimpse the heart of God. We do not always recognise the act of another which reveals God's presence in their life reaching out towards our own life. Peter found it difficult to allow Jesus to wash his feet. Peter was tempted to stand aloof. At first he did not recognise Jesus' portrayal of the compassion of God, so simple was it.

Read   John 13:1-17

There are many gracious and kindly actions performed with genuine love in the world. There are many simple, yet powerful moments which express not only care but also point towards the justice which God calls his human creation to live out. On this Holy Thursday, this Maundy Thursday, speak with one or two people about those signs of love and care which you have experienced from other people. Speak about simple actions which have not only described but also moved towards the justice which God demands within human community. There are many, yet we can be careless or too rushed to appreciate the divine action by which we are surrounded

Servant God, seen so clearly in Jesus washing the feet of his disciples, make us sensitive to those simple actions which speak of you and are of you.
Servant Messiah, you knelt at the feet of those whom you taught and led,
make us sensitive to those for whom we can simply show your love.
We pray for those who feel - and too often are - unloved, even within the Christian community;
> for those whose imagination disturbs us,
> for those whose lifestyle differs from ours,
> for those whose relationships are different from our expectations,
> for those whose bodies suffer from neglect,
> for those whose poverty undermines our comfort.
We cannot serve all. Show us, challenging Spirit, how we can serve,
for the love of Jesus.

Jesus' crown of thorns is set against a background representing the tearing of the Temple curtains, opening the way to God for all believers. The colouring of the original kneeler represents the wood of the cross, the stones of the Temple and new life from Jesus' resurrection.

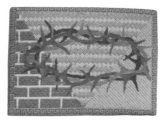

O God, who for our redemption gave your only Son to the death of the cross, and by his glorious resurrection has delivered us from the power of the enemy; grant us so to die daily to sin that we may evermore live with him in the joy of his resurrection. *(1549 Prayer Book)*

Read **John 18:1-19:42**

It's been too much to take in,
an exhausting week, very
tense, very intense. The
disciples didn't know what
was happening. There was
a chilling and deep fear.
Judas turned on Jesus.
Peter denied knowing Jesus.
Rumours abounded, and now they are real. I watched Jesus
being taken to Calvary.
I watched the sight of those terrible crosses, one, two,
three people gasping,
thirsting, dying, slowly, painfully, dehumanised. Life turning
into nothing, hope turning
into nothing. And the noise, noise of agony, noise of
disbelieving grief, the noise
of a crowd having a good time out, watching the spectacle,
and the noise of the soldiers
suspicious, nervous of the
atmosphere on this unholy
beginning to the holy day.
A haunting noisy silence.
Death, his death, silence.
I don't want to see that he
is dead, but I watch them
take him from the cross, from
that place. They take him for
burial. It is over. It really is
finished. And all that love,
that delight in people, that
pleasure in life, that passion
for life is finished, And all
that is holy and pure and
splendid is torn apart. I am
desolate. I am empty. I turn
toward nothing and no-one.

This Holy Saturday, this time of death in life
is lived by many in our society for many reasons.
As Mary and the others left the place of crucifixion they entered a place
of grief, which is a place of dark numbness, no feeling risked, no future dared.

> **Holy God, where have you roamed, why have you left your creation?**

The Hebrew people moaned in the wilderness.
What benefit is a grave in the wilderness over the graves of slavery?
By the waters of Babylon, they wept.
They couldn't sing to the Lord in a foreign land.

> **Holy God, ...**

There is no Gospel for today There is no good news.
There is no purpose. Today there is no tomorrow.
And yesterday is too terrible for memories to comfort.
There is a void, in me, in my friends, in the world.

> **Holy God, ...**

The desperate for food and drink cannot live before they die.
The elderly of our land dwell isolated in their homes.
The young hit out, to gain at least some human response.
And drugs numb the pain of rebel and polite suburbia.

> **Holy God, ...**

The heart sinks to a deep fear when I hear of illness,
cancer, HIV and AIDS, and cuts me off from friends and family.
My heart shrinks from those in the dark tunnel of mental torment.
There is this long waiting, this empty waiting for me and for them.

> **Holy God, where have you roamed, why have you left your creation?**
> **The heart cries out. Can it dream of crying out to you ever again, Holy God?**

Even churches with no other adornment usually make use of flowers. The madonna lily on this kneeler and its colours are a celebration of motherhood and the glory of the incarnation. They remind us of the part flowers play in our places of worship.

Give thanks for those whose provision and arrangement of the church flowers remind us of the beauty of God and of his world. Pray for those who cannot smell the fragrance or see this beauty, with its reminder of God's constant care for us.

Easter Day

Read John 20:1-18

It was Mary Magdalene who went to the tomb, she went by herself.
It was Mary Magdalene who went to fetch Peter and the other disciple.
But they left, They had seen the tomb. They waited for nothing else.
It was Mary Magdalene who stayed. She wept. She fought with her grief.
She struggled with angels. She interrogated the gardener. She wanted
to know.

Jesus said her name. 'Mary'. She lived again as her name was spoken.
Mary Magdalene turned to Jesus. 'Rabbouni!' She went to hug him.
Jesus, her friend, her teacher, her companion, her Lord - alive.
Naturally after the nightmare of separation, injustice and death,
she went to hug him, to hold him so as never to be separated again.

Jesus says: 'Do not hold on to me, because I have not yet ascended to
the Father.'
How hard those words sounded to Mary. After everything, she never
wanted to lose him.
Jesus turns her from the past to the future. 'Go and tell them ...'
Mary, the marginalised woman, went to announce Easter.
Courageously she looked to the future. He is risen!

Jesus is risen! Alleluia!
The gloom is lifted, but we are told not to hold on to him!
Holy God, help us to have Mary's nerve,
wrestling with angels, questioning and announcing Easter.
Give us the courage to speak, show and share Easter
with each other, with all the brokeness of the world,
not with a trite smile but with a deep passion
for the dignity of the human community, of each individual.
Give us such courage, that like the disciples we may hear
from the Marys of our world that tomorrow is for you to make.
May we not hold on to what comforts us,
but turn from what was;
towards what with you is still to be.

Pray with the **Union of Welsh Independents** *(Europe pages of the CWM prayer leaflet)*

The Union of Welsh Independents seeks for prayer for communities where many have lost their jobs in the steel and other industries, and for communities hurt by foot and mouth disease. Churches of the Union are starting to use a new Welsh language hymnbook, Caneuon Ffydd, *and ask that it may bring a new spirit into their worship and be a sign of oneness in the Lord.*

Read **John 20:19-31**

Thank you, Lord, for Thomas -
>not there,
>not sure,
>left out when the others saw the risen Lord.

Risen Lord, be with *us*, we pray, when *we* fail to see you;

when we want to believe
>but can only see legend and myth,
>and are tempted to put you away with other childish things;

when we long to be loved and accepted
>but feel forever outsiders, excluded from your embrace;

when we envy those who take for granted your close presence in
their lives
>while we feel nothing;

when in bereavement we crave the certainty of eternal life
>but are afraid it is simply wishful thinking.

Risen Lord, as you came to Thomas in his doubts,
offering him your cross-torn body,
come to us, we pray.
Reveal yourself afresh, that we too may say with Thomas:
"My Lord, and my God!'

Thank God for any neighbours you have who follow other faiths and for Christian neighbours who worship in other churches. Ask to be shown God's Spirit in them all, and pray for the breaking down of harmful barriers and the growth of our mutual understanding of God and his purpose for us all.

*Pray with the **Churches of Christ in Malawi** (Africa pages of the CWM prayer leaflet).*

Women and young people are increasingly involved at different levels in the church - women are now officially involved in preaching. The church asks for prayer for the training of preachers and pastors.

Read **Luke 24:13-35**

*The two disciples on the Emmaus Road were full of the events
of the previous few days, full of their hopes and dreams – and
disappointments; full, even, of the rumour of a living Christ.
And yet – they did not wait to see what was happening in
Jerusalem, they did not recognise Jesus as he walked beside them.*

*How often are we so preoccupied by our own agendas that we, too,
fail to see Jesus?*

Risen Lord: **break into our lives, and help us to see you afresh.**

When we are totally immersed in doing your work,
remind us to spend time with you.   Risen Lord: **break into...**

When we stock our shelves with other people's prayers,
surprise us and meet us in the very core of our being.
                              Risen Lord: **break into...**

When 'church' means meetings, money and plans for restoration,
reveal afresh the living community of those who love you.
Risen Lord: break into...

When we label people as 'problems',
help us to see the unique individuals you love.
                              Risen Lord: **break into...**

When we assume all those around us to be indifferent or hostile to you,
convince us once again with your good news, and empower us to
pass it on.
Risen Lord: **break into our lives, and help us to see you afresh.**

Risen Lord, break into our lives
Help us to look again into the faces of those around us
And to see you afresh.

Creche is the French word for a cradle, giving protection to the very young just as the Ark gave protection to Noah's family. Noah's Ark, with its animals, is often a favourite toy.

Pray for those who, in church creches, look after the very young so that their parents can take part in worship, remembering that the helpers sacrifice their own time of worship to give it to others. Pray for very young children, that they may find the church a place of friendly faces and words.

*Pray with the **United Church of Zambia** (Africa pages of the CWM prayer leaflet).*
Ordained in Samoa in 2000, the Revd Fereti Tutuila is now minister in charge of St Andrew's, Lusaka, the United Church of Zambia congregation whose worshippers include President Frederick Chiluba. Mr Tutuila says that an important part of his ministry is visiting members, 'especially those who haven't come on Sundays for ages'. He also takes many funerals because of the high death rate from AIDS, malaria and other diseases. He has held services in St Andrew's to talk about AIDS, in which people living with HIV told the congregation what it was like to be infected.

Read Psalm 23

This meditation explores the images of peace and security which Psalm 23 evokes, against the back-cloth of Easter. It is designed to be read antiphonally by two (or more) voices.

The Lord is my shepherd
I see the risen Lord - Cross-scarred, yet wonderfully alive!

I have everything I need
And as I come to accept that this prodigal outpouring of God's love is for me, I am given an inner peace.

He lets me rest in fields of green grass
Pictures arise, of beauty and a quiet serenity: the irises, daisies and buttercups of Iona in May.

and leads me to quiet pools of fresh water
- the limpid calm of a lake in summer

He gives me new strength
Images of tenderness and love –
all calming me, slowing my breathing, relaxing my knotted limbs

He guides me in the right paths, as he has promised
… bringing into a heightened focus
the God who is everywhere
– in his word, in creation, in others.

Even if I go through the deepest darkness
whatever happens to me now, wherever I go, I will find God there.

I will not be afraid, Lord
I will hold His torn hand, and be steadied.

For you are with me
I will feel the constant reassurance of his presence.

I know that your goodness and love will be with me all my life
I can believe a joyful homecoming awaits me

and your house will be my home as long as I live.
…for here and now,
even in the midst of time and space,
I have found eternity.

Debt is the unfinished business of the last millennium, says the World Development Movement. People in the 41 poorest countries in the world have got steadily poorer because of debts to wealthier countries incurred 30 years ago at low interest rates and intended to aid development. Interest rates have risen and now form an annual charge on these countries' budgets which dwarfs the amount they spend on health and education for their people. Development has been replaced by increasing poverty, illiteracy and ill-health.

Christians have played a long and effective part in identifying this debt and calling for its reduction and have joined with thousands of people around the world in peaceful, persistent and informed campaigning to have the debt forgiven. The issues are complicated by varying views on the role of the World Bank and the International Monetary Fund and by the difficulty of ensuring that selfish and inefficient governments pass on the benefit of debt remission to their people. Nevertheless Uganda, which has observed the conditions governing debt relief, is now spending around £25 million of cancelled debt payments to improve rural water supplies, increase food productivity, build classrooms and give free primary education to its children from the Poverty Action Fund it has set up.

Leaders of the world's eight wealthiest countries have agreed to the cancellation of £100 billion of debt for the 41 poorest countries, and about 12 billion had been written off by the middle of 2001. Together and individually, Christians continue to give time, money and prayer to ensure that this principled movement in world thinking does not lose any of its momentum. Jesus says, 'Anything you did for one of my brothers here, however insignificant, you did for me.'

St George may have been a Roman soldier martyred at Lydda for his Christian faith. He may have been a mediaeval knight who helped the Crusaders at Antioch. Part of his legend may have come from a bishop of Alexandria murdered in the 4th century.
Perhaps this mixture of origins makes him a fitting patron saint for a nation with many ingredients.

God of all peoples, help us to remember our past – good and bad –
                as we pray for our future.
Remind us that we have been both conqueror and conquered;
              that we have explored, colonised, traded and exploited –
but also, that we have received, sheltered, assimilated and been enriched by the people of many nations.

In the past, we have been ready to make great sacrifices for our principles:
Help us today, to continue to stand up for freedom for others, toleration and human rights.

In the past, we gained much of our prosperity through exploitation –
through conquest, slavery and industrialisation:
Help us today in a new millennium, to be at the forefront of moves for justice –
for fair trade, cancellation of debt and just and sustainable world development.

In the past, our society has absorbed many newcomers:
Help us today, to rejoice in the many colours and cultures,
which are so vibrant a part of our land.

Today we are reminded of St George of popular legend,
slaying his mythical dragon:
May we be inspired to confront and conquer the real forces of darkness,
until our kingdom grows to reflect your kingdom,
and becomes a place of peace and justice, love and harmony.

The red cross of St George
is also the cross of Jesus Christ, your Son,
who died, and lives, for all people.

Pray with the **Presbyterian Church of Wales** *(Europe pages of the CWM prayer leaflet) for increased sensitivity to the special needs of people with disabilities and for the newly-appointed chaplain to deaf people. Farming and the tourist industry in Wales have been badly disrupted in the recent past, affecting the lives and livelihoods of country-dwellers and the life of country churches.*

Praying with
CWM churches

2002

 Council for World Mission
a global community of churches

EUROPE

Reformed Churches in the Netherlands (RCN)
Pray that:
- The RCN may grow in faith in God, despite declining membership.
- The churches will not stay inward looking but take an active role in society.
- The churches will develop a vision for Europe in ecumenical cooperation.
- The RCN will attract more young people.

Congregational Federation (CF)
Pray:
- That individual congregations will develop a clear mission identity.
- For the response of churches to the vulnerable in society.
- For the effects of political and social devolution across Scotland, Wales and England.
- For the CF's church planting initiatives.

Presbyterian Church of Wales (PCW)
Pray:
- For dialogue to form a united free church.
- That congregations will be active in meditation, prayer and mission.
- For the success of the PCW's outreach to children and youth.

The Uniting Church in Penrhys, Wales, works with special needs children at a local school. The church includes all four CWM denominations in the UK.

United Reformed Church (URC)

Give thanks for:

- The creativity and vision of those embarking upon new initiatives in local mission.
- The faithful witness of congregations struggling with economic and social decay.

Please pray for:

- The synods as they support and challenge congregations in their life and witness.
- The church's members: their service sustains worshipping communities throughout the country.

Upper Clapton URC, in London, UK, hold their annual crusade.

Union of Welsh Independents (UWI)

Give thanks for:

- The enriching partnership of CWM.

Please pray:

- That churches bridge the widening gap between the generations.
- That the UWI will meet the needs of God's people as it seeks new ways of being a church.
- For creative educational programmes to prepare individuals for the Christian ministry.
- For the debate about uniting the churches in Wales.

EAST ASIA

Presbyterian Church in Singapore (PCS)

Give thanks for:

- The combined worship service which celebrated 120 years of the PCS in April 2001.
- The fundraising programmes for the missions schools and the theological seminary.

Pray for:

- Unity to grow through the synod theme: "United in love and service".
- The resources needed to train more full-time pastors and missionaries.
- The Presbyterian Community Services, working with children, the elderly and youth at risk.
- Greater cooperation between the English and Chinese presbyteries.
- More staff for the synod office to provide better communication between the churches.

Children at a Presbyterian Church in Singapore day centre.

Presbyterian Church of Korea (PCK)

Pray for:

- The mission to the unemployed, homeless, disabled, foreign migrant workers, hospitals, industrial areas, schools and prisons.
- The reunification of North and South Korea.
- Church planting in rural and island areas of Korea.
- The Women Ministers' Association, providing support to women pastors and counselling victims of domestic violence.

Gereja Presbyterian Malaysia (GPM)

Pray for:

- Wisdom for the national leaders to sustain peace and harmony.
- More full-time workers, and for the intercessory ministry supporting them.
- Lively and vibrant faith in the church.
- Improved training for counsellors and carers.
- The ministries to women and youth.
- The self-supporting projects, that they will be unaffected by the economic slowdown.

Presbyterian Church in Taiwan (PCT)

Pray for:

- Guidance and wisdom as the PCT and CWM's Pacific partners develop relations.
- The staff of the rehabilitation centres established following the 1999 earthquake.
- PCT congregations to respond to the increased rate of suicides.
- Stronger youth and campus ministries.
- The aborigine ministry in urban communities.
- Justice, peace and security between Taiwan and China.

Praying before a Sunday service at a Presbyterian church in Taichung, Taiwan.

Hong Kong Council of the Church of Christ in China (HKCCCC)

Please pray for:

- The people of Hong Kong facing economic recession and hardship.
- The election of a chief executive of Hong Kong.
- The HKCCCC missionaries around the world.
- Local churches to have a willingness to cooperate with the Chinese churches.

PACIFIC

Congregational Union of New Zealand (CUNZ)
Please pray that:
- The mission programme, "In Jesus' Footsteps", continues to uplift churches.
- Young people will develop a deeper commitment to Jesus Christ.
- Families and individuals will find healing and love through the ministries of the churches.
- The government of New Zealand will govern by the principles of the Lord Jesus Christ.
- The CUNZ shares the good news with those who are turning from God.
- Women's ministries will continue to develop, and more women will take up leadership roles.

Kiribati Protestant Church (KPC)
Pray for:
- The KPC's general assembly in September 2002.
- The Commercial and Vocational Centre, established to subsidise the church.
- The Women's Fellowship, as it provides practical training.
- The youth evangelism and Sunday schools, making the church relevant to young people.
- The KPC's education department, which is trying to establish secondary schools in neglected areas.
- Experienced financial staff for the KPC headquarters.

Congregational Christian Church in American Samoa (CCCAS)
Pray:
- That the church leadership will seek peace and truth in its decision-making.
- That the government will act honestly and justly in its duties and responsibilities.
- For those suffering because of crime and discrimination.
- For those who are homeless and without food and drink because of natural disasters.

Nauru Congregational Church (NCC)
Pray for:
- The new economic initiatives.
- Training of church leadership.
- The church's community work: visiting prisons, hospitals and the elderly.

Front cover: A Sunday school run by the Nauru Congregational Church.

United Church in Papua New Guinea (UCPNG)

Pray for:

- A fall in the high level of crime in a country that is 98% Christian.
- The leaders in the assembly and regional offices.
- A peaceful general election in 2002.

Presbyterian Church of Aotearoa New Zealand (PCANZ)

Please pray:

- For the new initiatives in working with children and young families.
- For improved communications through the new publication (sPANZ), email and internet.
- For the social, health and educational work with the Maori community.
- That the Council of Asian Congregations continues to contribute to the diversity of the Church.
- For lay training to be part of the vision of each parish in the church.
- For all staff and ministers who work to share the good news.

United Church in Solomon Islands (UCSI)

Pray for:

- The church's work to resolve the tension between ethnic groups.
- An end to the economic crisis in the country.
- The newly elected government following the October 2001 election.
- The centenary celebrations in May 2002 to mark the arrival of the gospel in the Solomon Islands.

Congregational Christian Church in Samoa (CCCS)

Pray for:

- Action to reduce global warming, which is affecting small Pacific countries like Samoa.
- Students on government and church scholarship programmes studying overseas.
- The CCCS missionaries currently working in Zambia, Switzerland, the Marshall Islands and Fiji.
- All those working to assist the Christian nurture of youth.
- The members of parliament and the government.

Ekalesia Kelisiano Tuvalu (EKT)

Pray for:

- The threat and effects of global warming.
- Full participation of women at all levels in the church.
- Enhanced use of the Tuvaluan language and musical tradition in the church.

SOUTH ASIA

Church of North India (CNI)

Pray for:

- Those helping the earthquake victims in Gujarat, and for the funds needed for rehabilitation.
- The persecuted minorities.
- The work of the synodical boards of health and social services.
- The training programmes organised by the church's Human Potential Development.
- The church's work among women and children.

Church of South India (CSI)

Pray:

- For the work against injustice and social inequality, especially among the untouchables.
- For Christians and other minorities persecuted by Hindu fundamentalists.
- That the church's campaigns will put the poor on the government's agenda.

An anti-Christian militant at a Hindu fundamentalist event in India.

Presbyterian Church of Myanmar (PCM)

Pray for:

- Better theological education for pastors.
- Lay leadership training.
- The church's evangelistic campaign.

Presbyterian Church of India (PCI)

Pray:

- That the words and service of the PCI will proclaim the gospel.
- For the spiritual renewal of church leaders, pastors and congregations.
- For the social and economic empowerment of the weaker members of society.
- For peace and harmony within the region.
- For the 35th biennial session of the assembly of the PCI at Kyrdem in April 2002.

Aizawl theological college, an institution run by the Presbyterian Church of India.

Church of Bangladesh (CoB)

Pray:

- That Christian families will live and raise their children in God's will.
- That the church serves people of other faiths with humility.
- For political peace and an end to violence.
- For women to be respected and have dignity in their work.

Health workers with local children at a church-run clinic in Kandi, Bangladesh.

AFRICA

United Church of Zambia (UCZ)

Give thanks for:

- The numerical growth of the UCZ.

Pray for:

- The programmes of the new Eastern Presbytery.
- The communication secretary, Moses Mbulo, and his new department.
- The theological college and its degree programme.
- The mission and evangelism secretary, Derek Silwenga, and the work under his care.
- The leadership of the UCZ.

Daily work on the United Church of Zambia's Chipembi Farming Institute.

United Congregational Church of Southern Africa (UCCSA)

(comprising synods in Botswana, Mozambique, Namibia, South Africa and Zimbabwe)

Give thanks for:

- Political stability in Botswana, Mozambique, Namibia, and South Africa.
- New ministry and mission projects within the UCCSA.
- The new Synod of South Africa.

Pray for:

- Spiritual renewal and faithfulness in the churches.
- The people of Zimbabwe, who face economic hardship and political uncertainty under the regime of President Robert Mugabe.
- The provinces in Mozambique affected by flooding.
- The new partnerships being formed to combat HIV/AIDS.
- The ongoing struggle to eliminate poverty and deprivation.

Churches of Christ in Malawi (CCM)

Give thanks for:
- The completion of the office block for the church secretariat and other tenants.
- The completion of the multipurpose hall in Blantyre to be used for women's activities.
- The interest young people are showing to join the ordained ministry.

Pray:
- For the new central council and the cooperation of the finance, projects and mission programmes.
- That youth and women's activities in the church will continue to flourish.
- That God will give strength and good health to retired ministers.
- For those that have lost homes and possessions in the floods.

Church of Jesus Christ in Madagascar (FJKM)

Please pray for:
- The church leadership to bring progress for the church and the nation.
- The project to fight fast-growing illiteracy.
- The development and fundraising projects.
- The fight against corruption and injustice.
- Spiritual renewal at every level within the church.

Uniting Presbyterian Church in Southern Africa (UPCSA)

(comprising presbyteries in South Africa, Zambia and Zimbabwe)
Give thanks:
- For the election of the UPCSA's first woman moderator, Rt Rev Diane Vorster.

Pray for:
- Church growth and evangelism.
- Community development with special concern for youth, the environment and HIV/AIDS.
- Leadership training, including lay training.
- Increased unity and reconciliation between the presbyteries.

© NICK SIREAU/CWM

Rastafarians at Mountain View informal settlement, South Africa, where the Uniting Presbyterian Church has an outreach project.

CARIBBEAN

United Church in Jamaica and the Cayman Islands (UCJCI)
Pray for:
- An effective response to violence and inner-city deprivation.
- Rehabilitation for drug abusers and prisoners.
- The mission outreach to drug addicts and prostitutes.
- Church planting.

A pupil at a United Church school in Jamaica. The church believes education offers a way out for the many socially deprived youths.

Guyana Congregational Union (GCU)
Please pray:
- For the principal and executive officers as they implement the strategic mission programme.
- That income-generating projects will provide economic growth and employment.
- That young women will get involved in the Women's Union.
- That young and old will seek ways to bridge the generation gap.
- For political stability, and that this will cut down racism, discrimination and unemployment.

Council for World Mission, Ipalo House, 32-34 Great Peter Street, London SW1P 2DB, UK
Tel: +44 (0)20 7222 4214   Fax: +44 (0)20 7233 1747 or +44 (0)20 7222 3510
Email: council@cwmission.org.uk Website: www.cwmission.org.uk
Charity No 232868 registered in the UK
Printed by Healeys Printers, Ipswich, UK

*If we focus on God as Creator, we may find God distant and remote.
But if we focus our thoughts entirely on Jesus, then we may lose the
sense of mystery and divinity.*

Read John 14:1-14
which points to the unity of Father and Son.

Spirit of the Living God, present with us now: Show us the Father.

You are Creator,
infinite and eternal,
at whose Word, matter, universe, life sprang into being;
Maker of all we know – and all we have yet to discover;
utterly beyond our imagining.

And yet, Father,
you heard the cries of the Israelites in Egypt;
you revealed yourself to Moses and talked to him face to face;
you rescued your people.

Spirit of the living God, present with us now: Show us the Son.

You were a vulnerable baby,
born in a chosen place, and in calendar time,
utterly dependent for food, warmth and comfort;
toddling steps and babbling sounds.
You died, bloodied and broken, stretched helpless on a cross.

And yet, Jesus,
death could not contain you.
You returned,
re-creating for us a way to God.

**Spirit of the living God, present with us now,
help us to see
the Father in the Son,
the Son in the Father
and you in both.**

Ask God for light and love in all the ministerial training colleges which serve the Church, thanking him for learned teachers and motivated students. Maintaining college courses of high quality for comparatively small numbers of students has faced the colleges and their governing bodies with difficulties and challenges in recent years. Pray that the decisions which have to be made will always witness to God's abundant grace and spread his good news.

Read John 14:15-21

In C S Lewis' children's classic 'The Lion, the Witch and the Wardrobe', Aslan (the lion) breathes on the statues – those who had been turned into stone by the witch. In the cartoon film version, this is an especially powerful image, as cold grey stone turns visibly pink, and comes back to life under Aslan's breath.

Come, Holy Spirit,
and breathe on me.

Breathe on my slow mind,
that I might grasp something of the eternal truth of God.
Breathe on my frozen heart,
that I might feel the infinite love of God,
        for me – as I am – now.
Breathe on me and release me,
that I might respond,
with the whole of my being,
to your love –
by loving others,
and sharing with them the joy,
        the love,
        the peace
which the Spirit has breathed into me.

Come, Holy Spirit,
and breathe on me –
and bring me new life in Christ.

Heavenly Father, you have given to your people the true Bread
that comes down from heaven, your Son Jesus Christ; grant that our souls
may be so fed by him who gives life to the world, that
we may live in him and he in us; and your Church be filled with the power
of his unending life.

Read Acts 1:1-11

*On Ascension Day, just as at the tomb, in that moment of
bewilderment where
the future was swallowed up by uncertainty, two Men in White
appeared:*

> *Why do you look for the living amongst the dead?*
> *Why do you stand looking to Heaven? they asked.*

The response is obvious, but perhaps the answer less so.

*The women, the disciples, looked for Jesus in places they thought
him to be and could not find him, but the Men in White challenged
their assumptions.*

Almighty God, we too have moments of bewilderment;
where the future of our lives,
of the church,
of our nations,
seems swallowed up by uncertainty.

When we also look for you in places we knew you to be
and cannot find you,
may we hear the challenge of the Men in White today:

> *Women of Glasgow, men of Birmingham,*
> *Why do you stand looking at the empty pews?*

> *You are witnesses;*
> *You are to share your experience of Jesus' good news*
> *with the world.*
> *You are an extension of Jesus' work, his body on earth.*

> *O men of Brecon, women of Galway*
> *Why do you look for the living amongst the dead?*

Open our ears, Breath of life,
to hear and respond to the challenge of your Men in White.

Remember those leaving home for the first time, to study or to work; that, away from the fellowship they have grown up in, they may know God's continuing closeness to them. Many may not easily find a spiritual home in their new place and will need to draw on reservoirs of faith filled in earlier years. Some will face loneliness and will be tempted to return home; ask for good friends for them. Pray for parents with emptier homes, that they may grow closer to each other and learn how to strengthen and encourage those who have gone away.

Pray for the work of Christian Aid, its staff members and its partners around the world; that it may everywhere help the needy to eat well, the homeless to be sheltered, the weak to live, hungry minds to be filled and justice to be done; in our name and in the name of Christ.
Pray for those who collect, and those who give.

Christian ⁝⁝ Aid

Read Acts 1:6-14; 1 Peter 4:12-14, 5:6-11;
John 17:1-11

*Moving house... retirement... moving school... changing job...
bereavement... ageing...
There are some changes we choose; others are forced upon us.*

*Did the disciples want Jesus to go and the Holy Spirit to come?
Did the recipients of Peter's letter want to continue suffering?
Did Jesus want to ascend to Heaven and leave the disciples?*

Change is an essential force of life:

> *Spring*
>
> *Summer*
>
> *Winter*
>
> *Autumn*

*There is no growth without change,
no deeper dive into the pool of eternal life.*

> Breath of life and wonder,
> when we, like the disciples,
> like Peter's readers,
> like Jesus,
> are plunged into the depths of the unknown,
> grant us the courage of love to overcome our fear.
> Help us not to spend all our energy
> trying to escape from where we find ourselves;
> but to swim with the unpredicted currents,
> to marvel at your wonders, new to us,
> and to find treasure in the depths of your eternal life.

On the Whitsun kneeler the dove of Jesus' baptism is surrounded by the flames which were seen on the disciples' heads when they received the Holy Spirit at Pentecost..

O God, who on the day of Pentecost fulfilled your promise to pour out your Spirit upon all humanity; shed abroad on your Church in every race and nation the gifts of that Spirit, that through the preaching of the gospel your glory may be shown clearly to all people.

Like a flame

Pentecost

Read Acts 2:1-21; 1 Corinthians 12:3-12

Spirit of God
swooping and soaring freely across the earth;
sometimes breezing, sometimes gusting,
sometimes gentle, sometimes violent,
sometimes resting, sometimes swooping through.

Dancing like a flame,
with streaming rainbow tail and song beyond beauty,
you touch and spread your many different colours,
scatter your myriad notes
wherever you go;
as you spin your rainbow and weave your song
into the heart of the world.

Spirit of God, empowerer,
touch and lead us, your world today;
draw us together,
that as our colours unite in contrast and beauty,
as our voices chord and discord in rhythm and harmony,
the world may be filled
with your glory and your song of life.

Think of members of your congregation in mid-career, maybe maintaining a workload which is burdensome or putting strain on their family life. Remember those upset by change or the threat of change; those for whom life has lost its novelty or challenge, as well as those who find their life and work continually fulfilling. Pray for those whose life is upset by illness, for those facing redundancy and unemployment, that they may continue to find healing love, steadiness and security in God and in the church family.

Read **Genesis 1:1-2:4a; Psalm 8; Matthew 28:16-20**

Holy Weaver of life,
you honour us
by choosing us as your threads to work with.

You have
enabled us through your Son
enriched us with life
enhanced us with love
equipped us with hope
energized us with joy
entrusted us with responsibilities
engaged us in mission
empowered us with your Spirit.

Holy Weaver,
knit together our skills and abilities,
unite in pattern our dreams and hopes,
blend and contrast the colours of our experience and
traditions,
that together we may create and be created into
the wondrous tapestry of life you hold in your mind's eye.

Pray for those you know facing retirement, willingly or unwillingly. Ask that they may find relaxation without losing their interest in life, that they may find pleasure in new and different undertakings, a new vision of God. Pray for those whose pace of life is slowed by illness or disability, those who have lost life partners, and those whose strength is stretched by caring for partners who are disabled. Remember those now dependent on others, that they may find help and accept it graciously, and those who lack and long for the company of other people. Thank God for all those who visit and support the old.

Read **Romans 1:16-17, 3:22b-28; Matthew 7:21-29**

Good news! God has a gift for us,
for our families, our communities, for our nations.

It is a gift which is freely given;
which enables us to believe all shall be well - eventually;
which finds forgiveness for our darkness and enables us to forgive;
which reveals to us that we are loved and enables us to love;
which shows us our value and the value of others;
which gives courage;
which gives purpose;
which brings healing.

This is the gift of salvation...
for you,   for me,   for the world.
Good news indeed!

Gracious God,
Words cannot express our gratitude for your great gift.
Help us never to take it, or yourself, for granted,
but to express our gratitude
by allowing your good news to soak through our lives,
so that we may live it out and share it with the world.

May it become so much a part of us
that, in difficult times, we do not set aside our faith
like last season's fashion,
but discover the reality of the life you give more fully.

Gracious God,
may your gift be received and celebrated
in the hearts and minds of our nations,
our communities, our families, ourselves,
today and always.

Pray with the **Presbyterian Church of Aotearoa New Zealand** *(Pacific pages of the CWM prayer leaflet).*

The general assembly of the Presbyterian Church of Aotearoa New Zealand will decide in 2002 whether to make its Presbyterian Pacific Islanders Synod a permanent body. Former Synod Moderator Le'i'ite Setefano said that the synod, set up in 1998, had enabled Pacific islanders scattered in different congregations to speak with a strong voice.

Read **Genesis 12:1-9; Romans 4:13-25;**
Matthew 9:9-13, 18-26

Lord, sometimes, like Matthew in his custom-house,
we seem to spend lifetimes in little boxes:
narrow horizons, narrow churches, narrow faith.
We, too, need your inviting word:
Come! Follow! Leave your boxes!

Call us, Lord, and give us faith
to risk being your disciples;
to risk being open to new possibilities with you;
to risk the kingdom's festive party where there are
no 'us' and 'them' but each belongs and celebrates;
to risk your forgiveness and mercy.

For this is your good news, Lord: all sheer grace,
all about belonging and needing, not about deserving.

As it was for Abraham, so it is for us:
leaving our 'familiar country',
breaking free,
trusting the promise of God,
allowing the energy of God's grace to work its
miracle within us - even in old age, even today.

This is Jesus' touch of healing; this is resurrection!

So, let us come, follow, leave our boxes.
And let's all party!

Genesis 18:1-15, (21:1-7)
Psalm 116:1-2, 12-19
Romans 5:1-8
Matthew 9:35 - 10:8

'Ask the plants of the earth, and they will teach you'

Zimbabwe is a country with which the United Reformed Church's Commitment for Life programme has direct links. Through Silveira House, a Christian institution with a wide variety of skill training programmes, subsistence farmers learn how to cope with water scarcity, to raise their crops in a way friendly to the environment and to make money from their smallholdings which will pay for school fees and health care.

Edson Mashudhu, coordinator of the Silveira House sustainable agriculture programme, has written: 'In permaculture we work with nature, not against it. We encourage chameleons, along with bees, wasps and other insects to do various jobs for us rather than using chemicals...'

O God whose heart is rooted in our earth,
give us minds to question the practices that harm it.
Show us the detailed threads linking life to life,
And make our hands delicate to tend our plants with care.
Janet Morley

Amid the conflict and tension of recent months in Zimbabwe, Silveira House has offered a conflict resolution course, whose members are seeking to become peace-makers. New work at the House on traditional medicines and herbs aims to bring health to many and reduce hospital costs in a deeply impoverished country.

Pentecost 4

Read **Romans 5:1-8; Matthew 9:35 - 10:8**

'Harassed and helpless' and Jesus was 'moved'.
Twenty centuries and more of the stories of faiths
do not seem to have changed things very much:
refugees, asylum-seekers, people seeking shelter,
protection, safety, healing, compassion, loving embrace -
even within their own homes, even among their own.

Move us, Lord, with your compassion;
      not pity that feels sorry
      but entering into others' pain,
      listening to their story,
      holding their hand,
      sharing their tears,
      moved by their anger,
      engaging with harassing powers,
      empowering helplessness,
      confronting evil.

Commission us, Lord, by name,
to your kingdom's tasks:
      proclaim,
      heal,
      raise,
      cleanse,
      drive out.

Only such costly engagement could be proof of love
and crucible of hope for you, Lord. And for us too?

Pray for those who are considering church membership in an age when commitment seems more difficult. Their vision and courage in asking to be received is considerable; pray that the congregation will be encouraged to live more closely as the body of Christ, to demonstrate his life to the newcomers and to be open to the gifts they have to offer.

Read **Genesis 21:8-21; Romans 6:1b-11;
Matthew 10:24-39**

*'I will not have this slave-girl's son sharing the inheritance with my
son Isaac.'*

*'No one is worthy of me who cares more for son or daughter than
for me.'*

Lord, sometimes the choices are impossible:
> our past can haunt us;
> the failures of others can wound us;
> the tug of love can fracture us;
> our loyalties can test us;
> the power of forgiveness is stretched to the uttermost.

Yet, Lord, we have faith that at the heart of such struggles is your
promise:
> you receive the child of slavery as your son;
> in desert testing you are with us;
> knowing our secrets, you embrace us in our failures;
> hidden powers cannot kill the soul, the depths of our being;
> if we lose our life for your sake we will gain it.

So let us not be afraid, Lord, and call us to new discipleship:
> buried with Christ in baptism, raised with him,
> call us to new life;
> since what we have been, our struggles and choices,
> has been crucified with him,
> set us free to be alive to you, in Christ Jesus.

Pray for people considering a call to Christian ministry. Ask that God will deepen their understanding of themselves and of him, and that they may find wise friends and counsellors to question. Thank God that he continues to call us all to his service, and leave time in your prayers for him to speak to you. Pray for those who staff inquirers' conferences and vocation conferences or who are consulted individually, that God will give them wisdom and discernment and a balanced confidence in his leading.

*Pray with the **Congregational Union of New Zealand** (Pacific pages in the CWM prayer leaflet).*

Now in the midst of a five-year mission programme, the Congregational Union of New Zealand has special concern for the deeper Christian commitment of teenagers and young adults. It maintains healing ministries for sufferers from child abuse, alcohol and drugs, neglected marriages, unemployment and poverty.

At God's disposal

> **Read** Genesis 22:1-14; Romans 6:12-23;
> Matthew 10:40-42

Testing commitment is all very well, Lord,
but isn't disguising murder as sacrifice a bit much?
Isn't this taking the principle of caring more for you than
for son or daughter a bit far, Lord?

Yet at the back of our minds there is this nagging reminder:
'When Jesus calls a person he bids them come and die.'
Were Abraham and Bonhoeffer right
and we just cannot take it?
Perhaps discipleship is as hard as this!

At least, Lord, teach us that there are no easy options
        if we are to be at your disposal,
        if we are to be implements for doing right,
        if we are to walk the way of holiness,
        if we are truly to embrace eternal life.

And open us up to your grace,
        to extend hands of acceptance,
        to hear the challenging word,
        to recognise goodness,
        to exchange cups of water,
        to become channels of human simplicities,
knowing that such small things
can be ultimate tests
for your disciples.

Young people and young adults can find a valuable centre of friendship as well as learning within a church group and in the congregation. The kneeler shows their hands linked around the Bible.

Pray for the older children in Junior Church, in youth fellowships and teenage groups, who need to find good values and standards among their peers as their ties with their family lengthen. Many of them will find other loyalties competing with the church fellowship in their next few years; pray that a good seed is being sown in their lives now.

Read **Genesis 24:34-67; Romans 7:15-25a;**
Matthew 11:16-19, 25-30

*Spirituality... is the passage of a people through the solitude and
dangers of the desert, as it carves its own way in the following of
Jesus Christ. This...is the well from which we must drink. From it
we draw the promise of resurrection.*   Gustavo Guttierez

Lord, we know of desert places within us, around us:
    where the journey of faith can be hard,
    where we cannot find beauty and loveliness,
        where the search for love goes unrewarded,
        where the well-spring of the water of life seems dry.

Deserts can be within us, in the depths of our lives:
        they can touch us, in intimate relationships;
they can be around us, in the despair and hopelessness
        of communities;
they can be beyond us, as nations and powers exploit,
        oppress, wield injustice.

Lord, as we carve our way through deserts
    be present in your loving beauty in Jesus,
    reveal to us the loveliness of your glory,
    captivate us with the grace of your love,
        release us from loads too heavy to bear,
        and put upon us the easy yoke of your law of love.

Rescue us from our wretchedness!
Let us draw from the spring of the water of life
the promise of resurrection!

Pray with the **Presbyterian Church of Myanmar** *(South Asia pages of the CWM prayer leaflet).*

'Illiteracy is a major problem in Myanmar,' says Presbyterian Church of Myanmar mission secretary Lalengzauva. The church already runs an extensive communication training programme that promotes social development through literacy and skills training, and over the next few years it aims to boost its Christian outreach through education.

Encourage us, God,
it is easy for us to lose heart,
to be dis-couraged.

Discouragers abound.
Some look into the church from the outside,
wondering
in heaven's name
what we are doing,
questioning the meaning
of our worship
and work.

More disheartening
are those who look out from the inside
watching the gales of change
sweep away the familiar landmarks,
worrying about declining membership,
complaining about people of promise
for whom faith never took firm root,
asking whether the sowing of gospel seeds
has been worth
time
effort
energy.

En-courage us, God,
give us new heart
in the work of your harvest,
knowing deep down
that in your economy,
sooner or later,
harvest-time will come,
generous and overflowing.

Pray for Churches Together Fellowships in which our churches are linked in towns and cities of England, Scotland and Wales. Ask that the fellowship may not be an extra burden on small or busy congregations but a tangible strength for shared Christian witness and social concern, a meeting-place which enlarges our understanding of Jesus Christ.

Pray with **Kiribati Protestant Church** *(Pacific pages of the CWM prayer leaflet).*

The islands which make up Kiribati are suffering from recurring droughts, storms and soil erosion as sea levels rise, presumably from global warming.

Read Matthew 13:24-30, 36-43

God within us and around us,
good and evil grow together in your world
like wheat and weeds in the harvest field.
Their roots are hidden,
interwoven,
entangled;
yet their fruits are visible.

Evil is a mystery
challenging us with unanswerable questions.

Evil has a subtlety,
often disguising itself as good.

Evil spoils, divides,
twists, distorts,
corrupts, betrays,
crucifies,
and seemingly thrives.

Evil encounters us
in our world,
our nation,
our church,
ourselves
but never overcomes.

God made known to us
in the crucified and risen Jesus,
empower us as we seek justice in your world;
give us patience and faith to trust you,
knowing that in your time
all will be well.

The keyboard, organ pipes and ornamental trumpets on this kneeler sing silently of the musical life of the church.

Thank God for the gift of music (remembering also those who do not appreciate it) and for those who have given us hymns, songs and instrumental music which move us and lift our spirits. Pray for organists and pianists, sometimes longing for greater skill; for church bands and for the singing of the congregation, that our best efforts may know God's acceptance.

*Pray with **Nauru Congregational Church** (Pacific pages of the CWM prayer leaflet).*

Past concern about damage caused to Nauru's environment by phosphate extraction during the former Australian administration has been overtaken by concern about damage to the economy as phosphate reserves are exhausted.

Faith the size of a mustard seed

Read Matthew 13:31-32

A man and woman
with their two young children
came to the city centre church in Derby.
It was Tuesday, early evening.
The doors were locked
but the caretaker who lived over the shop
saw them.
When the minister arrived
their tale unfolded.
They had made a long journey
before they reached the empty flat
round the corner from the church.
All they had was in two large bags,
clothes and precious possessions
and twenty-five pounds in cash
to buy food (and furniture?)
Someone had pointed them to the church;
it was their place of hope.

In three days
a group of people
of great faith, little faith and no faith
had done a lot of small things
so that a family from Serbia
could find themselves at home.

In your upside-down kingdom, Lord,
remind us
that small things work great miracles;
and help us to do them.

Pray with the **United Church in Papua New Guinea** *(Pacific pages of the CWM prayer leaflet).*

Papua New Guinea's economic problems have prompted the United Church's women's groups in two districts to learn basic skills in sewing, weaving, crochet and other crafts which can generate income. The classes are hosted by Kadeboro Circuit Women's Fellowship, whose chairperson Arage Sere said, 'the aim is not to make a profit but to earn a living.' Workshop participants pass on their skills when they return to their villages.

Read **Matthew 14:13-21**

Pray for particular people and/or places you know about after each verse.

Loving God
help us to be Christ to all those
whose lives touch ours.

May we see others
as Jesus did,
with eyes of compassion.

May we listen,
as Jesus did,
to the cries of broken hearts
and a broken world.

May we reach out to others,
as Jesus did,
with healing and hope.

May we serve others,
as Jesus did,
with no strings attached.

May we break bread with others,
as Jesus did,
that the hungry may be fed.

May we celebrate with others,
as Jesus did,
your abundant provision.

Loving God,
help us to be Christ to all those
whose lives touch ours.

Pray with the **United Church in the Solomon Islands** *(Pacific pages of the CWM prayer leaflet).*

The Solomon Islands have been torn apart by violent ethnic conflict and by a continuing economic crisis. The violence has upset the work of the United Church in the Solomon Islands, says acting general secretary Wilson Gina, and the economic crisis has led to a fall in its income. Still the 50,000-member church is planning to build its third hospital to relieve heavy pressure on the country's medical system, is providing training for school drop-outs and is emphasising strong pastoral work among disaffected people as a way towards solving the conflict.

Read 1 Kings 19:9-18; Matthew 14:22-33

At day's dying
as the light slipped into night,
you carved out from your crowd-encircled ministry
the lonely place
and holy space
where you had room
to be renewed in your Father's will.

> Christ of the quiet mountain,
> teach us the meaning of prayer,
> the art of praying.
> Tune our ears
> to the tones
> of your still small voice,
> a sound of sheer silence.

At day's dawning
you came to storm-battered disciples
afraid of the deep
and the danger
and the dark.

> Christ, ruler of wind and waves,
> teach us to speak your words
> to the fear
> and faltering faith
> of those
> around us
> all at sea.

Pray with the **Ekalesia Kelisiano Tuvalu** *(Pacific pages of the CWM prayer leaflet).*

Tuvalu is one of many Pacific island groups which could be completely submerged if global warming raises the sea level only a few metres, says Ekalesia church president Eti Kine. Already storms eroding the coast are severely damaging agriculture and fishing.

Read Genesis 45:1-15; Romans 11:1-2a, 29-32;
Matthew 15:21-28

This is hardly believable, Lord:
    the brother sold into slavery is Pharaoh's counsellor;
brothers who sold Joseph to passing traders
are loved and embraced still;
those who jealously abandoned
are welcomed with kisses and tears.

Help us, Lord, to see, to know,
to feel - with tears and kisses - what we cannot believe:
    your miracle of transformation and energy of forgiveness,
    your kisses of welcome and tears of acceptance.

Lord, help us to see that it cannot be all in the mind;
it must be in the heart, too, 'strangely warmed'
    by Gospel good news!

**God, convince us anew that you have not rejected
your people:**
    **day by day you release us from prisons of disobedience
    into the promised freedom of your mercy.**

**Convince us that this promise is for all: all imprisoned,
all shown mercy.**

**Grant us, Lord, the courage of the Canaanite woman to insist
that your Gospel is not for special people
but for all who come crying out their need only,
trusting faith to be enough.**

Let this be so for us and for all.

Church stewards provide the initial welcome to regular worshippers and visitors alike, symbolised by the handshake.

Think of those who come to your church looking for company, friendship, a place to think and a place to pray. Pray that stewards will be sensitive in their welcome, helpful representatives of the whole congregation.

Pray with the **Congregational Christian Church in Samoa** *(Pacific pages in the CWM prayer leaflet).*

With the widest possible mission vision, the Congregational Christian Church in Samoa has been working with CWM member churches in Zambia, Jamaica and the Cayman Islands and the United Church of Christ Congregational in the Marshall Islands. It is planting new congregations among Samoan migrants in New Zealand, Australia, Hawaii and continental USA.

Pray with the **Congregational Christian Church in American Samoa** *(Pacific pages in the CWM prayer leaflet).*

Read **Exodus 1:8 - 2:10; Matthew 16:13-20**

What a beginning for a chosen people!
The vocabulary of cruelty tells it all: task-masters;
        oppression;
forced labour; grinding down slaves; making life bitter;
        harsh demands;
ruthlessly using; 'if a child is a boy, kill him... throw him
        into the Nile.'
Threats to powerful thrones have to be dealt with,
        controlled.

(Are we really hearing an ancient story? It sounds familiar!)

And out of this catalogue of oppression and injustice
a reluctant leader emerges - hidden in a rush basket,
floating in a reed bed, drawn out of the water,
chosen by God.

Perhaps true courage and tenacity, true hope and faith,
do not come through ease but through testing:
        forged in the crucible of oppression,
        shaped by grinding down,
        drawn from dangerous waters.

After all, even Rocks like Peter know fragility.
Millennia of rain and wind and ice can shatter solidity;
storms of self-doubt, stubbornness, denial, faith too fragile
for water-walking, shape apostles too.

They know that the vulnerable are raised,
that their strength is in their weakness,
that fragility and certainty together build the church
on the foundation of One whose garden of resurrection
blossomed from the rubbish heap of death.

On such tested foundations build and rebuild us,
shape and reshape us for costly discipleship.

*Pray with the **Church of Jesus Christ in Madagascar** (Africa pages in the CWM prayer leaflet).*

Enjoying a rewarding involvement in rural development - farming, caring for people's health and the environment - the Church of Jesus Christ in Madagascar works for the restoration of God's creation in the country's natural reserves and forests.

Read **Exodus 3:1-15; Matthew 16:21-28**

God of holiness,
> present in the wilderness,
> the angel in the burning bush,
> the voice calling from the fire,
you make this place holy,
you call us to tread it gently:
Spirit of God, enable us to see,
empower us to follow.

God of liberation,
you see the misery of peoples and hear their crying,
you know their suffering and come for rescue and release,
you call us to be partners in liberation:
Spirit of God, enable us to see,
empower us to follow.

God whose name we know:
I am who I am, I will be who I will be,
whom we can trust tomorrow because we have
> known you today,
whom forebears knew and addressed by name,
whom we know in Jesus, Emmanuel, God with us:
Spirit of God, enable us to see,
empower us to follow.

Jesus, son of man, suffering servant,
walking the *via dolorosa* to cross and death,
raised to life again, set free from death,
calling us still to take up our cross, to renounce self
and follow you for life's sake, for the world's sake:
Spirit of God, enable us to see,
empower us to follow.

Pray with **the United Church in Jamaica and the Cayman Islands**
(Caribbean pages of the CWM prayer leaflet).

United Reformed churches in Britain are making a Commitment for
Life to seven partners in **Jamaica** who are working for better
health, education and training and the lifting of tens of thousands
out of a life damaged by poverty and violence.

In the downtown area of Kingston, the capital, several thousand
people live in shacks of scrapboard and zinc sheeting, where there
are few and poorly-paid jobs and family school fees may equal the
whole of a parent's earnings. The S-Corner Community, named
from a sharp bend in the road, runs a Happy Club where children
can do their homework in safety, a Grassroots College for school
drop-outs, health clinics for mothers and babies and old people,
and a scheme to help families to build 'VIP' toilets which work
without access to the sewage system.

International debt is at the root of many of Jamaica's problems and
the Jamaican Council of Churches has a project to monitor the
benefits of debt cancellation if and as it happens. New world trade
regulations which threaten the loss of guaranteed markets for
Jamaica's bananas may add to the country's poverty.

O God, whose word is fruitless
when the mighty are not put down,
the humble remain humiliated,
the hungry are not filled and the rich are:
make good your word and begin with us.

Open our hearts and unblock our ears
to hear the voices of the poor
and share their struggle;
and send us away empty with longing
for your promises to come true
in Jesus Christ.
Amen

Janet Morley

Read Matthew 18:15-20

Holy God, we live in a world of many disagreements. It's the stuff of soap operas. It's the delight of political commentators. Sometimes, when looking at the TV or reading newspapers, it would seem that the disagreements are all that matters. Harmony isn't newsworthy, it isn't the stuff of gripping drama.

Lord, forgive us an unhealthy preoccupation with the disagreements of others.

When two people fall out, when one complains about the other, when an argument becomes public there's the temptation to fuel the fire, to fan the flames. There's the temptation to shelter from the tensions in our own relationships by hiding in the pain of others coping with the agony of battle.

Lord, forgive us if we rejoice in the disagreements of others.

You, God, show us a different way of behaving towards one another in the life and ministry of Jesus. You ask us to look at each other as sister and brother, because we are each your child. You teach us to listen and speak with respect for the other. You show us the courage to be with the other. You call us to the mission of making peace.

Lord, give us the patience to ask how you would listen in the tangles we make.

You trust the church to be a maker of peace. This is extraordinary when we consider its divisions and the damage it has caused. The Body of Christ is to draw people together, to create harmony and justice. Keep firm in us the vision of being together in a way which is good for each, and in which each is blessed by the other.

Lord, build up the Body of Christ, that we its members may be your light to each other and to your world.

And when we fail:

Inspire us to try again in the spirit of the banquet which is your kingdom.

*Pray with the **Guyana Congregational Union** (Caribbean pages in the CWM prayer leaflet).*

The Guyana Congregational Union continues to pray for spiritual and numerical strength for its witness to Christ, in a nation facing severe economic difficulties and heavy unemployment. In a single recent year, this country of 750,000 people saw 10,000 Guyanese leave for the USA and 4,800 for Canada.

Read Matthew 18:21-35

We want to be safe with you, O God.
We tend to justify ourselves, we like to think that we are pleasing
to you.
Yet deep down we know there is such a gap between how we are
and how you call us to be.
Yes, we speak for justice. We collect for the poor. We recoil from
poverty and hopelessness in
the lives of others.
But we want to be safe. We want you to keep us safe.

Like the king's servant we would battle for our own survival. We
hurl ourselves on your grace. We demand more than mere justice
for ourselves. We expect you to be gracious; prodigal-like we
assume your embrace.

We are not wholly good or bad. We plod along hoping we do and
give just about enough. And yet, there's that nagging, disturbing
knowledge that still people suffer because of us, still people die
whilst our wealthy nations prosper.

**May we look at our sister and brother in need as we know you
look at us.
May we dare to say aloud, there but for the grace...**

(silence)

Dare we imagine ourselves in third world poverty?
Dare we feel the shivering of the homeless in the shop doorway?
Dare we weep with the tears of the socially excluded?
Dare we gasp at the stings of our own prejudices?

(silence)

**May the timidity within us be overcome by your compassion
bursting through us.
Today, help us seize the chance of being like the servant's king.**

The traditional harvest offerings of bread, fruit and vegetables are shown on this kneeler.

Thank God for the renewal of the seasons and for the seeds which grow in secret, yet upon which all of us rely. Confess our misuse of the earth, and pray for wisdom in the face of changing climate and weather patterns, and a loving resolve in our hearts to end the world's hunger. Pray for farmers and market gardeners, wholesalers and shopkeepers, and those who control the world's trade, that they may work for the common good.

Read **Matthew 20:1-16**

Remember those playground parades?
Two 'captains', picking their teams,
the rest in line, trying so hard to look fast and keen -
potential goal scorers! great goalkeepers! - trying so hard to be
chosen.

Was it like that in the market place?
A huddle of men, striving to impress:
trying to look young, strong, tough, nimble –
the sort of person who would do a job well.
Only this time, the stakes were not popularity or pride
but a whole family's daily bread.

Standing for hours, without being picked.
Which was worse: to wait through the heat of the day, with hope
gradually dying?
Or to go back to a hungry home empty-handed, admitting failure?

Then work! With only an hour left, to impress,
to ensure a job for tomorrow!
Working with such a will, all tiredness forgotten!
What a surprise!
A full day's pay – for an hour's work?
O, thank you, Lord.

(2 voices)
1 Loving God: we thank you, that you do not choose only the fit,
   strong, and talented,
2 *not only the weary or despairing.*
1 Your prodigal love is rich and overflowing,
2 *there is enough for all of us – and to spare.*
1 We are infinitely valuable in your sight,
2 *each one of us uniquely precious.*
Generous God, we thank you.

Hold in your prayers all those who have accepted a call to ministry. Be alert to the needs of those ministers and church workers you know personally, remembering our ministry to each other in the body of Christ. Pray for church-related community workers, and for all social workers in our communities, that God will strengthen them in difficult and demanding situations and give them encouragement through the wellbeing of the communities in which they work.

Read **Philippians 2:1-13**

Creator of all that is
- you entered your created world,
born as a baby.

Source of all wisdom and knowledge
- you laid aside divine knowledge, and accepted the restrictions
of human age, human ability, and the customs of the time.

Eternal and Immortal
- you submitted yourself to the everyday limits of a human life,
and the ultimate necessity of a human death.

Whole and complete in yourself,
you took the risk of becoming dependent,
of needing, relying on and trusting others.

Lord, your whole nature and essence is love;
yet you exposed yourself to the weak and cowardly;
to the self-centred and self-seeking; and to those with hate and
anger in their hearts.

Self-emptying Lord,
you gave up everything
to enable us to see you and know you;
and in knowing you, to be transformed,
changed from glory into glory... lost in wonder, love and praise.

Scrabble is a popular board game which can be used to maintain fellowship with folk unable to get to church. 'Mobile' church members play against housebound members in a Scrabble league. The slightly scrambled text on the kneeler is from Psalm 119, verse 103.

Pray for those who miss the fellowship of the church because they can no longer attend worship. Give thanks for church folk who have devised ways of restoring the fellowship and give their time to make it work, through giving lifts to church, through the tape recording of services for distribution, through Scrabble leagues and visiting programmes.

Read Philippians 3:4b-14

I think I understand what Paul meant, Lord.

I too have watched athletes before races -
gazing, with inner concentration and total control,
visualising the race ahead.
Their start perfected by constant repetition;
muscles bulging from intensive exercise;
stamina built up through long years of development.

And that look: absolute focus
a zealous hunger for success
everyone, everything else, excluded from their minds.

Yes, I can see what Paul meant
and have to ask myself:
am I that single-minded,
am I that wholehearted, in following you?

Lord Jesus, help me so to love and follow you
that my life is centred on you,
that everything I think, and feel, and do
is an offering to you.
Not for my pride or satisfaction, Lord Jesus,
but to your eternal praise and glory.

Give thanks for local preachers who serve so many churches, especially the smaller ones, and whose willing faithfulness is so important to the whole Church. They need God's help in understanding the changing needs of the congregations they visit, and discipline and opportunity to study the gospel they preach. Many of those who offer for this ministry are older people. Ask God to give them freshness of thinking and vigorous spirits through which his Spirit may continue to work.

Read Philippians 4:1-9

Listening God,
if you were Prime Minister,
head of a business or school,
GP or jobbing builder,
you would be so hedged about with protocol and civil servants,
secretaries and receptionists,
that we would need to make an appointment days, no, *months* in
advance
to be allowed just a few moments of your time.

And yet you -
Creator and Sustainer of all that is -
you make yourself freely available to us, all the time:
a 24 hour connection, and no answer-phone!
You urge us to come to you in prayer.
And so: we ask...we seek... we knock.
Rejoicing in your nearness, we bring our needs to you.

(time and space for silent or spoken intercessions)

Listening God,
We have brought to you
our heartfelt and most urgent desires;
and we are at peace,
knowing that you have heard.

In **Bangladesh** the United Reformed Church's Commitment for Life programme has a partner in the Christian Commission for Development (CCDB). The commission works with the poorest people in Bangladeshi society in a wide range of programmes including health care for rural mothers and children; providing small loans, education and training; and disaster preparation, shelter building and giving emergency aid.

Let us hold up before God the land and people of Bangladesh,
giving thanks for its ancient culture and traditions
and its still-new sense of nationhood and parliamentary democracy.
Let us celebrate the beauty of Bangladesh,
its vigorous energy, the strength of family life, the hospitality of
its people
and their resilience in the face of so many dangers and difficulties.

In concern for its great need, let us pray for the whole people
as they live with the natural cycle of cyclones and floods
that bring the boon of enriched soil and abundant water
as well as the grave threat of wind, flood and tidal waves
made worse by the 'silent disasters' of river erosion and
global warming.

Pray for the Government of Bangladesh and all who work to strengthen the economy and reduce poverty;
for agencies working to combat the natural arsenic poisoning of water sources;
for the Christian Commission for Development in Bangladesh and its staff;
for its programmes to increase literacy, develop skills and support rural development.

The click of a mouse,
a bit of plastic:
it doesn't seem like real money any more, Lord!
And yet the same choices remain,
between your way, and Caesar's.

Clothes: designer labels to flaunt and impress;
yet hiding what misery, what illegal practices?
Sweatshop labour, under-age employment?

Ripe, juicy oranges, refreshing and healthy;
yet grown, perhaps, on stolen land?
And irrigated with stolen water?

Tea, coffee, chocolate: we joke about 'needing' them, to keep us
going.
What about the growers?
Do they earn enough to keep *them* going?

Flowers - surely they must be safe enough?
Except for the labourers, required to use toxic sprays
with no protective clothing.

So it still comes down to the same choices, Lord:
your way or Caesar's?

Lord, help us to make our choices wisely.
Help us to use our money to create real change,
to establish your kingdom values, of dignity, fairness and justice
for all.

The open book which is the background to the four figures represents education in general and also the Bible. The figures represent different age-groups of children within the church.

Pray for all who work with children in the church, that they may meet the wonder and excitement of childhood with lively signs of God. Pray for the children, that the church may be a place of discovery and love for them, and especially for children whose life is unhappy. Ask for energy and freshness for all those who make the church's children their concern for Christ's sake. Remembering present-day anxiety about children's safety, pray that children's workers may be protected from false accusations.

Read Leviticus 19:1-2, 15-18; Matthew 22:34-46

(for alternating voices)

Gracious God, we come to you
because first you came to us in Jesus.
We come with many questions on our lips,
for we live in sceptical, doubting times.

We find truth spun in many different ways
and certainties so hard to hold on to.
In our hearts we would be faithful people
but soon find ourselves shifting position.

What is the secret of faith in such times,
how can we love God, and neighbour as self?
For some it is an exercise of will
for others it's the gift of your Spirit.

For us can it be the way that we live?
Honouring God with honesty, justice.
Honouring neighbour with care and respect?
A creed of conduct, divinely inspired?

'Love God entirely, and neighbour as self'
Jesus instructs us to live out our lives.
Come close to us Christ, help in our weakness,
inspirer of faith, strength of your people.

Pray with the **Presbyterian Church of India** *(South Asia pages in the CWM prayer leaflet).*

Zaidazauva is a CWM missionary in Taiwan who comes from the Mizo people of north-east India, where the Presbyterian Church of India is one of the most dynamic churches in the world. Pastor to a small congregation of the Presbyterian Church in Taiwan, he is leading its members in the friendship evangelism practised in his home church in Mizoram, helping them overcome their normal diffidence in adding three new members each to their own church every year - by meeting new neighbours, sharing the gospel with them and inviting them to church to find out more.

Read **1 Thessalonians 2:9-13; Matthew 23:1-12**

'The proper glory of God is men and women who are fully alive'

St. Irenaeus

'For God is at work in you who believe' 1 Thessalonians 2:13b

Life-giving God,
sustainer of every breath we take,
you bid us breathe deeply of the
oxygen of your word, so that
refreshed by that life-giving air
we may be renewed for your work

for you are at work in us this day.

Inspiring God,
when we prefer the stale heavy air
of convention, tradition and
habit, shut into ourselves,
merely existing, not being the church,
let the gale of your spirit blow

for you are at work in us this day.

Love-giving God,
cherisher of everything that breathes,
your atmosphere invigorates,
encourages and challenges,
teach us to trust you more, that we
may not fear adventuring out

for you are at work in us this day.

10 November
Remembrance Sunday

Joshua 24:1-3a, 14-25
Psalm 78:1-7
1 Thessalonians 4:13-18
Matthew 25:1-13

Think of those in your church or community for whom remembrance of past and continuing conflicts is painful; who have lost loved ones, partners, family, in wars or acts of violence. Pray that we discover how to use times of remembrance for healing, reconciliation and peace-making within ourselves.

*Pray with the **Church of South India** (South Asia pages of the CWM prayer leaflet).*

Students and staff at the United Theological College of the Church of South India in Bangalore have a deepening relationship with a community of 300 street-dwellers in the city. The street-dwellers are included in the college's Christmas and Easter celebrations, and college members protested with them when the government tried to clear them from the streets in the name of cleaning up the city.

Read **1 Thessalonians 4:13-18**

'Let me rise
With the wise
Counted in their number' (Rejoice & Sing 57)

It's said that that every time we sleep
we rehearse our deaths.
However wise that sounds
I doubt if many of us think that.
We are like children as we sleep,
needing to refresh, recover, recharge ourselves with energy,
preparing ourselves for the next day's (or night's) activity.
Unable to defend our selves from any assault
we lie helpless,
trusting that protected and secure
we shall be defended from all
perils and dangers and rise again
recreated, renewed, released.
So I prefer to think of sleep
not as a rehearsal of death,
but as an act of faith,
that whenever I rise,
and wherever I go
I shall find myself
within the boundaries of the Kingdom.

May God be with us
this day, and every day,
this night and every night
always.

Pray with the **Church of Bangladesh** *(South Asia pages of the CWM prayer leaflet).*

In a country with low levels of literacy and a general need for more education, regularly ravaged by natural disasters, the Church of Bangladesh is working for the spiritual and social development of all people. Living as a Christian in a predominantly Muslim nation is not easy, says Bishop Barnabas Dwijen Mondal. 'We have to show that our faith is relevant here and that Christianity is not a foreign faith imported from the West.'

Read **Matthew 25:14-30**

I have received little from God   **Have you?**
and so I have little to give back,
to pass on to you.

What little I have I keep safe,   **Is it?**
a responsible steward's response
to unknown demands.

Can I take risks with my future,   **You have**
endangering loved ones relying
on my safekeeping ?

I demand little from others,   **You do**
I force no one's hand, place no burdens
on those who are poor.

You cannot condemn me like this   **I do**
for my lack of adventure, my choice
to keep what I have.

What then can I do to make up   **Too late...**
for my conduct, in seeking to please
God whom I worship?

**In gratitude for all we are, O God,
and all we can achieve
we offer ourselves in your service.**

Pray with the **Church of North India** *(South Asia pages of the CWM prayer leaflet).*

With other churches and aid agencies, the Church of North India (CNI) is instantly involved when there is an earthquake disaster like the one which hit the region around Kutch early in 2001. The CNI opened five centres within hours of the earthquake to feed people who had lost their homes and those evacuated from quake-damaged buildings. In the heavily damaged village of Vijapasar, the ecumenical Action by Churches Together agency provided tarpaulin sheets and blankets for over 400 families.

Read Matthew 25:31-46

When the far-off final moment becomes
a close reality,
then we shall know
how often,
unaware and ignorant,
we have encountered Christ :
whether we have cared for
or neglected him,
deliberately, consciously,
carelessly, or accidentally.
Why this is so the gospel story
does not say.
It is a mystery.
Perhaps it is to test us
so that we are not able to discriminate
between those Christ loves and those we love?
Surely it must be more than that :
for such a test will find all lacking,
and God knows that.
No, the mystery remains.
We have to live with the knowledge
that we cannot always know
what we do is right.
We have to live in faith.
We have to risk ourselves
for others to know Christ.

Be our faith's teacher, O God, our judge and our deliverer.

According to the Eastern tradition Andrew is the first called of the disciples. His martyrdom by crucifixion at Patras (on the gulf of Corinth) has been associated with the X shaped cross which forms part of the saltire - the flag of Scotland. Much legend surrounds Andrew and a number of apocryphal writings are ascribed to him. His bones and relics are said have travelled widely - to Constantinople (Istanbul) in 357, from there in the 13th century to Amalfi in Italy, with his head taken to Rome in the 15th century (returned to Greece by Pope Paul VI in 1964). The history to which Scots are inclined tells of the bringing of St Andrew's relics and bones to the place now known as St Andrews, Fife in 347 by St Regulus.

In 760 Angus, King of the Picts, adopted the blue and white cross of St Andrew as his standard. Legend claims that St Andrew appeared to Angus in a dream on the eve of a great victory against the Northumbrians at Athelstaneford in East Lothian. An important shrine to St Andrew grew up at Kilreymont in north-east Fife in the ninth and tenth centuries. In time St Andrew displaced earlier Celtic saints as the patron of the Kingdom of Alba (Scotland to be). St Andrew was probably promoted by kings such as Constantine II (900-943) who used the saint as a means of unifying his Scottish and Pictish peoples into one nation.

Russia also claims St Andrew as patron saint by virtue of missionary work done round the Black Sea.

John Young

This meditation draws on the strongly practical aspects discerned in Andrew's character, set against the claims of numerous churches to possess parts of his bones and relics, the contrasting character of extrovert brother Peter, and the 'smeddum' (commonsense, spirit) Andrew displayed (according to John's Gospel) in responding to Jesus' call to discipleship.

Andrew,
it's a long way from Bethsaida of Galilee
(and just as far from Russia)
to end up as patron saint of Scotland,
land of the mountain, glen, and flood;
it's just as well you cared little for the accidentals
like bones, for there's more of them in churches
than ever you needed on earth.

Andrew,
fisherman first, but always brother of Peter
(did you ever need reminding?)
you must have had the patience of a saint
to put up with yon man each day ;
its just as well you cared little for blether and bluster,
preferring the truth of what a person
does to what he says he will do.

Andrew,
disciple first of fiery John and then Jesus,
(what smeddum you had to choose him);
how sound your judgment was when you followed
the call to fish in new waters.
It's just as well you remind us that the church's mission
is to do likewise, in the sure knowledge
we'd prefer to stay where we are.

Gracious God
we thank you for the example of Andrew
whose actions spoke louder than words,
whose patience led others to Jesus,
whose courage as martyr we mark
on this his feast day.

Acknowledgements

Prayers on right-hand pages in this Handbook are by the following authors:

Fiona Bennett - prayers dated 2 December to 25 December and 9 May to 2 June
John Slow - prayers dated 30 December to 27 January and 14 July to 11 August
Noel Davies - prayers dated 10 and 17 February, 1 March, 9 June to 7 July and 18 August to 1 September
John Young - prayers dated 3 March to 25 March and 27 October to 30 November
John Humphreys - prayers dated 3, 13 and 24 February, 26 March to 31 March and 9 September to 19 September
Meriel Chippindale - prayers dated 7 April to 5 May and 22 September to 20 October

Material on left-hand pages, gleaned from issue no 21 of ***Inside Out***, the CWM magazine, and used with permission is by Christo Lombaard (on Charity Majiza), 23.12.01: Richard Chong, 24.2.02; Nick Sireau, 21.4.02; Rainer Lang and Anto Akkara, 24.11.02; by Janice Jones, 16.12.01, from issue no 20; Nick Sireau, 3.11.02 from issue 22. Other items are from ***Inside Out*** and from CWM Info, a free internet news service: details from kenwyn@cwmission.org.uk The CWM website at www.cwmission.org.uk gives details of these and other resources, including free feature articles.
16.6.02 and 8.9.02 by Janet Morley, Commitment for Life worship material 1999.

1 March - Michael Ramsey from *Be Still and Know*.
Permission sought.

Kneeler designs which illustrate the cover and several pages of the Handbook are used by permission of **Naomi Hart** and Lion Walk URC, Colchester.